COLP and COFA: Compliance in Practice

Third Edition

TRACEY CALVERT

Commissioning editor
Alex Davies

Managing director
Sian O'Neill

COLP and COFA: Compliance in Practice, third edition
is published by

Globe Law and Business Ltd
3 Mylor Close
Horsell
Woking
Surrey GU21 4DD
United Kingdom
Tel: +44 20 3745 4770
www.globelawandbusiness.com

COLP and COFA: Compliance in Practice, third edition

ISBN 978-1-78742-919-2
EPUB ISBN 978-1-78742-920-8
Adobe PDF ISBN 978-1-78742-921-5

Contents

Executive summary

The authorisation regime in which all SRA-authorised law firms must appoint a Compliance Officer for Legal Practice (COLP) and Compliance Officer for Finance and Administration (COFA) was a by-product of the many changes introduced into the legal landscape through the Legal Services Act 2007. The roles became operational in 2013. This is now a well-established regulatory requirement.

Having taken on these roles, COLPs and COFAs should be working within their firms to ensure that both the business, and everyone within it, are meeting all of their collective and individual regulatory obligations. The compliance officers must integrate their roles as effectively as possible within their firms and assert their authority to ensure that there is a positive response to regulation and the establishment of an effective compliance culture. The role requirements, and the obligations that go with them, are only set out in high-level terms in the Solicitors Regulation Authority (SRA) Standards and Regulations (the StaRs), and the detail of the individual firm is largely determined by the role-holders and their firms.

This book aims to de-mystify the roles, and to offer practical support to help COLPs and COFAs identify and meet the SRA's requirements, and to use their position to bring benefit to their firms. This new edition has been fully updated to deal with changes to the SRA regulatory regime, which took effect with the introduction of the STaRs and in line with guidance and risk management resources that have been published by the SRA. It contains useful materials for compliance officers on the knowledge and experience that they need, suggestions for systems and similar, which will demonstrate compliance in practice and support a consistent internal response, and also addresses the role of other members of the firm and the support that compliance officers should expect from them.

The COLP and COFA roles are set against a backdrop of recent unprecedented change in the legal services market and the way these services are regulated. The SRA now regulates not just traditional law firms, but also alternative business structures (ABSs) with non-lawyer managers and owners. To prepare for this change and to meet the consumer-focused objectives of the Legal Services Act 2007 (LSA), the SRA made radical changes to the way it regulates and with regards to what it expects from law firms. COLPs and COFAs need to fully understand the SRA's approach. First and foremost, the SRA has introduced and established principles-based and risk-based regulation. From the firm's perspective, this means looking more clearly at the culture of the business, and whether this facilitates the output of ethical legal services for each client, and at an effective management regime that supports the provision of client services and the adoption of appropriate behaviours by all managers and employees.

From the SRA's perspective, the focus is on risk-based regulation where the emphasis is on identifying how well firms are managed and, as a result, the level of risk they pose to their clients, to the public, and to the profession. The SRA views the COLP and COFA roles as pivotal to facilitating the right environment, driving up standards, and reducing risks to regulatory objectives. The role holders, alongside the firm's owners and managers, are their firm's primary link with the SRA in an era in which much more openness and cooperation is expected between regulator and regulated. The SRA has been swift to emphasise what it expects in this regard by initiating disciplinary proceedings against individuals and firms that fail to make full disclosure about issues affecting their COLP and COFA, or who do not otherwise cooperate with the SRA.

In many firms, the COLP and COFA have discovered that a major culture change is required in order to ensure that managers and staff are more alert to their regulatory obligations and to risks to compliance. Other key issues, such as how the compliance and risk management roles work in practice within the firm's management structure, are being put to the test. This book takes a comprehensive look at all aspects of the COLP and COFA roles. It starts with the legal and statutory provisions that define them, an explanation as to who can undertake the roles, and information on what the Rules require of them. It then drills down in more detail into the fundamental requirement to take all "reasonable steps" to ensure compliance and clearly explains what this means in practical terms.

This book clearly sets out what might comprise a compliance plan and provides advice on how risks to compliance can be identified and dealt with. Because firms now have to identify and record all non-compliance, it looks at ways this can be done and, importantly, at what might constitute "serious non-compliance", which needs to be reported to the SRA immediately (and which has been the subject of much anxiety for compliance officers). It also looks in some detail at the way the SRA has developed its position as a proportionate, risk-based regulator and, accordingly, identifies what firms can expect with regards to the way in which they will be regulated. This will include looking at the SRA's approach to risk and how it deals with firms it identifies as representing an unacceptable risk. Knowing how to achieve a low-risk rating is one of the main tasks of the COLP and COFA.

Because the COLP and COFA have different areas of responsibility for regulatory compliance, the book breaks down these roles into separate areas and looks at the detail of what is required for each in terms of systems and procedures. In relation to the COFA role, the Accounts Rules are examined in some detail. For the COLP, the SRA Codes of Conduct are the main focus of attention. For both roles, the importance of accommodating the SRA Principles is also considered.

Finally, the book looks at the personal position of the COLP and COFA. It examines the extent of their responsibilities against that of the other partners or directors, how their role fits within the firm, and at sources of help for compliance officers.

Key features include:

- A clear outline of the responsibilities of the COLP and COFA,
- Guidance on how these roles might fit into the management structure;
- Information on what a compliance plan should contain;
- Advice on what taking all "reasonable steps" to ensure compliance means in practice;
- Guidance on reporting non-compliance and what "serious non-compliance" might include;
- Details of the relationship between the SRA and the COLP and COFA; and
- Information on the SRA's approach to risk and its supervision regime.

Case studies, real life examples, and commentaries are also included where relevant.

About the author

Tracey Calvert is founder and director of Oakalls Consultancy Limited, which provides regulatory compliance, consultancy, and training services to lawyers and law firms. Tracey is a lawyer and a regulatory, compliance, and ethics specialist providing a variety of advisory services to members of the solicitor's profession. She is a regular speaker and trainer on these topics and has delivered presentations both within the UK and internationally.

Tracey is the co-chair of the International Bar Association's Professional Ethics Committee and is on the editorial board of the Law Society's Legal Compliance Bulletin. She is a contributor to *Cordery on Legal Services* and has written several books on compliance and ethics. Tracey was previously employed by the Law Society and the SRA as a senior ethics adviser and a policy executive. She has also worked both in private practice and in an in-house role.

Acknowledgement

Throughout this book, reference is made to the Solicitors Regulation Authority and its Standards and Regulations. We are grateful to the SRA for its permission to reproduce extracts as shown. For more information on the SRA, please visit www.sra.org.uk

Chapter 1: The requirement to have a COLP and COFA

Introduction to roles

The fact that it is necessary for law firms authorised by the Solicitors Regulation Authority to appoint compliance officers should not be a surprise to anyone reading this book. The concept was introduced in the Legal Services Act 2007 (LSA), translated into SRA language with the SRA Handbook 2011, and launched onto the solicitor-led membership in 2013.

Every law firm that is authorised and regulated by the SRA must have a Compliance Officer for Legal Practice (a COLP) and a Compliance Officer for Finance and Administration (a COFA) – or a head of legal practice and head of finance and administration if the firm is an alternative business structure – as a condition of authorisation. Losing a compliance officer is highly likely to have difficult regulatory repercussions.

But why do we need these roles? In this chapter we set out the origins of the COLP and COFA roles and explain why they were introduced. Whilst this is information that you may choose not to share with colleagues, it is nonetheless useful to understand why these roles were created and the responsibilities they carry. Being a COLP or a COFA carries with it an expectation that the role-holders will fulfil significant regulatory duties.

Brief background to the Legal Services Act 2007

The roles have their origins in the LSA and in order to understand why this is so, it is helpful to acquire a little knowledge of this piece of legislation.

The LSA has shaped the regulation of the legal services market in England and Wales and has a direct impact on how we provide legal services. It is not an exaggeration to describe it as a revolutionary piece of law-making.

Revolution was needed to open up the provision of legal services and to promote competition, flexibility of practice style, and consumer choice. It was also needed to build in some much-needed consistency in the regulation of all legal service providers, and to provide appropriate oversight and checks and balances.

The headline changes that were facilitated with the LSA were:

- The creation of the Legal Services Board as a super-regulator overseeing front-line regulators (bodies described as approved regulators), and with powers designed to ensure that these bodies complied with duties contained in the LSA when fulfilling their functions;
- The separation of representation from the regulation of a professional group;
- The requirement for regulatory bodies to be approved;
- The creation of regulatory objectives and professional principles that apply to the work and initiatives of the approved regulators and all authorised persons;
- A statutory framework to allow non-lawyers to be licensed to provide reserved legal activities (i.e., those legal services protected by statute, which can be provided only by qualified persons) through entities called alternative business structures (ABSs); and
- The creation of a single body to consider consumer-style complaints about the services provided by all legal service providers; the Office for Legal Complaints.

Latest figures released by the SRA indicate that over ten percent of authorised law firms are now ABSs. It is the development of ABSs that is responsible for the compliance officer regime. This is because ABSs can operate with minimal lawyer input whilst providing reserved legal activities such as activities relating to litigation, conveyancing, and probate services. The LSA was drafted to ensure that the fundamental ethical and professional principles that have always underpinned the delivery of these, and more broadly all other reserved and unreserved legal services, by traditional law practices run by lawyers and mainly employing lawyers, remained part of the character and ethos of all varieties of entities providing legal services.

One of the mechanisms for supporting this goal was a requirement in the LSA for all ABSs to have a head of legal practice (a HOLP) and a head of finance and administration (a HOFA). Section 91 of the LSA sets out the HOLP's duties and section 92 sets out the HOFA's duties in respect of the "licensed body" in which they are employed. This reference to "licensed body" is a description of an ABS-style authorised practice and is a term used by the SRA in its authorisation processes.

The legislative text requires the HOLP and HOFA to "*take all reasonable steps to ensure compliance with the terms of the licensed body's license, and as soon as reasonably practicable, report to the licensing authority any failure to comply with the terms of the license*". The terms of the license include a duty to ensure compliance with the licensing authority's rules by the ABS itself and also by everyone connected with it such as its owners, managers, and employees. The HOFA has responsibility for ensuring compliance with rules made by the licensing body in respect of accounts and the HOLP has responsibility for compliance with all other rules relevant to the body's license.

The HOLP must be an "authorised person" such as a solicitor or qualified lawyer. In this way, the LSA has created a system in which compliance rests with an individual who is qualified in the provision of one or more of the reserved legal services being provided by the ABS. This implies that they will have suitable subject knowledge and also will have been trained in the relevant regulatory and ethical requirements and be familiar with the standards required.

The creation of the roles gives regulators specific individuals within an ABS with whom they are legally entitled to have compliance conversations.

Further statutory protections include requirements that the HOLP and HOFA nominees must have consented to their designation and must be approved (albeit some individuals with an existing relationship with the regulator are deemed approved) by the regulator. This is designed so that the role-holders will be undertaking their compliance responsibilities willingly and knowingly and that the regulator has the opportunity to vet them to ensure that they are suitable candidates for the role.

Role of the SRA

The largest approved regulator is the Solicitors Regulation Authority (the SRA). The SRA is the independent and approved regulator of the solicitor's profession in England and Wales. It regulates solicitors of England and Wales and it also has powers to authorise and license law firms in England and Wales.

It is answerable to the Legal Services Board (the oversight regulator) and must ensure that its work is consistent with the LSA, and in particular the regulatory objectives and the professional principles described in this Act.

It is not a representative body; this is the role of the Law Society of England and Wales. Nor does it handle consumer complaints; this is the responsibility of the Office for Legal Complaints (sometimes described as the Legal Ombudsman or LeO). Instead, its remit is to ensure that solicitors and law firms conform to the high professional standards that it sets, to supervise and to take enforcement action as needed against individuals and law firms that fail to meet these requirements.

As an approved regulator and as a licensing body, it has been the SRA's responsibility to draft rules that will support this regime. More widely, this new role meant that it needed to review pre-existing rules and regulations and refashion them to suit the requirements of modern regulation in the LSA era.

It drafted the SRA Handbook in response to these requirements. In this work, the SRA wanted to create a single set of regulations that would apply without distinction to both ABSs and also more conventional and traditionally composed law firms. For this reason, the SRA took the HOLP and HOFA roles that were specifically and exclusively designed for the ABS market and decided to apply the concept of compliance officer appointments and tasks to all law firms, regardless of type.

Authorisation conditions dictate that every law firm authorised by the SRA must have a COLP and a COFA – in other words, a compliance office for legal practice and also for finance and administration. Changing the legislative titles slightly (from HOLP to COLP etc.) was deliberate and designed to make it very clear that the role-holders were to focus on compliance-related issues.

This was transformative for many law firms. Part of the rationale for doing this was because the SRA had concerns that some solicitors and some law firms did not engage with regulatory requirements in an appropriate way. By adding titled compliance officers and developing its rule book to show what a suitably-run law business looks like, the SRA's intention was to change attitudes to regulation, improve the relationship between regulator and regulated individual or entity, and to promote the development of compliance cultures in which compliance in practice was demonstrated and evidenced, and which fostered working environments in which ethical behaviour was supported.

The SRA Handbook was replaced by the SRA Standards and Regulations (the STaRS) in November 2019. The compliance officer roles have remained and the role-holders, together with the owners and managers of their businesses, continue to be in the regulator's spotlight. In ways that may surprise some more seasoned practitioners, the SRA involves itself in understanding how the authorised business is run. For example, the latest themes of this nature involve the SRA in considering how it can ensure that workplace wellbeing is accommodated within its regulatory framework so that it can use its supervisory and enforcement powers where it considers that the workplace environment does not facilitate professional behaviours.

Key extracts from Standards and Regulations that explain the authorisation process for compliance officer role-holders

The SRA Authorisation Rules set out the SRA's arrangements for the authorisation of law firms that are categorised as recognised sole practices, recognised bodies (solicitor-owned and managed law firms), and licensed bodies (ABS law firms) and collectively described as "authorised bodies". These Rules are part of the STaRs, which can be accessed at www.sra.org.uk.

Rule 8.1 of the SRA Authorisation Rules contains the requirement that all authorised bodies must have an individual who is designated as its COLP and an individual who is designated as its COFA, and whose designations are approved by the SRA.

Rules 8.2 and 8.3 add more detail to this starting point, as follows:

"8.2 *Subject to rule 8.3, an individual who is designated under rule 8.1 must:*
- *a) Be a manager*[1] *or employee*[2] *of the authorised body;*[3]
- *b) Consent to the designation;*
- *c) Not be disqualified from acting as a HOLP or HOFA under section 99 of the LSA; and*
- *d) In the case of a COLP, be an individual who is authorised to carry on reserved legal activities by an approved regulator.*[4]

8.3 *An authorised body is not required to comply with rule 8.2(a) where an individual who is designated under rule 8.1:*
- *a) Is currently approved by the SRA as a compliance officer for an authorised body with a manager or owner in common with the body; and*
- *b) Is a manager or employee of that related authorised body."*

In other words:

- The COLP and COFA roles cannot be outsourced to a specialist service. The reference to "manager" is to the sole principal, a director of a limited company law firm, a member of a limited liability partnership law firm, a partner in a partnership, or in relation to any other body, a member of its governing body. The reference to "employee" means an individual who is either engaged under a contract of service by a person, firm, or organisation or its wholly owned service company; or is engaged under a contract for services, made between a firm or organisation and that individual; or an employment agency; or a company that is not held out to the public as providing legal services and is wholly owned and directed by that individual, or under which the person, firm, or organisation has exclusive control over the individual's time for all or part of the individual's working week.

- The COLP must be a lawyer of England and Wales, a registered European Lawyer, or registered with the Bar Standards Board under Regulation 17 of the European Communities (Lawyer's Practice) Regulations 2000.
- The role-holder must not be disqualified from acting as COLP or COFA (such as would be the case if the SRA used its disciplinary powers to prevent an individual from fulfilling a particular role in the firm).

Approval of role holders

The SRA Authorisation Rules state that compliance officers (and new managers and new owners) must be approved by the SRA before accepting their appointments, unless they satisfy the "deemed approval" criteria.

The reason for compliance officer approval is obvious and because these role-holders have specific responsibilities in connection with the firm's regulatory relationship and the oversight of matters that relate to the firm's continuing authorisation. As we will see later in this book, they are expected to be the main point of contact with the SRA notifying the regulator of matters of relevance. This expectation requires a certain robustness and an understanding of the need to be individually, and on behalf of the firm, open and transparent and accountable.

These roles provide reassurance to the SRA that the decision to authorise individuals and entities to be legal services providers is a good decision and does not compromise consumer protection or public interest objectives. The SRA must be satisfied that the compliance officers in situ are of a suitable character to safeguard regulatory objectives. For this reason, approval is a prerequisite except in circumstances where the individual is already authorised by the SRA, or has been previously approved as a role-holder, and will be deemed to be fit and proper to be a COLP or COFA.

To meet these criteria, the individual must satisfy the requirements of rule 13.5 of the SRA Authorisation of Firms Rules and:

- Be a lawyer and a manager of the firm;
- Not be a compliance officer of any other authorised law firm;
- Not be subject to a regulatory or disciplinary investigation, or adverse finding or decision of the SRA, the Solicitors Disciplinary Tribunal, or any other regulatory body; and
- Your firm must have an annual turnover of £600,000 or less.

If the prospective COLP or COFA meets all the criteria, and the firm satisfies the turnover requirements, approval is a notification process. This is completed by the submission of a form to the SRA confirming that the individual is deemed fit and proper. The firm's records will then be updated to show the role-holder's new title.

Approval process for individuals who are not deemed approved

For obvious reasons, individuals who are not able to satisfy the deemed approval criteria will be subject to greater pre-appointment scrutiny by the SRA so that the regulator can satisfy itself as to the suitability of the proposed role-holder.

The application process is longer, and it makes sense to ensure that sufficient time and resources are allocated to the process. The SRA aims to make most role-holder decisions within three months from the date of submission of a correctly completed application. It will endeavour to reduce this to 30 days if the application is deemed low risk but the period can be extended to six months in some higher risk circumstances.

A firm that operates without a COLP and COFA is in default of the SRA Authorisation Rules and whilst there are emergency provisions to cater for unavoidable situations, such as the sudden death or incapacity of an existing role-holder, there are very few other circumstances in which the SRA will understand or sympathise with a gap in coverage. The firm will be expected to factor in sufficient time to ensure that there is continuity.

The application process for a new non-deemed COLP or COFA is designed to seek out information that enables the SRA to satisfy itself that the individual is sufficiently senior to discharge their responsibilities and to be able to report serious matters to them in an unfettered way. The SRA will want to be satisfied that the role-holder has suitable experience, knowledge, and support with which to fulfil their duties. The SRA also expects completion of a character and suitability assessment.

If the SA believes that the candidate is suitable, then it can approve them unconditionally. However, the SRA also has the option to grant approval with conditions or to refuse the application.

Rule 3.2 of the SRA Authorisation Rules states the circumstances in which approval with conditions may be granted. In other words, this caters for the situation in which the SRA considers that any risks posed by an applicant can be managed with conditions imposed on them and/or the firm. Rule 3.3 states that these conditions may specify that certain requirements must be met or must be taken by the firm; restrict the carrying on of particular activities; or prohibit the taking of specified steps without its approval.

Refusal of an application will occur if the SRA is not satisfied about the suitability of the candidate such that there are public interest risks to accepting a particular individual as a role-holder. Examples of circumstances that might trigger this decision include an applicant with a history of dishonesty, or a history of non-compliance with regulatory requirements, or where approval with conditions will not manage the underlying risks in a suitable way.

Individual role-holder and ongoing transparency requirements

Rules 13.10 and 13.11 of the SRA Authorisation of Firms Rules collectively create the requirement that an approved role-holder (regardless of whether they were previously deemed approved or not) has an ongoing regulatory duty to notify the SRA promptly of any information that is relevant to the SRA's assessment of their character and suitability.

This notification duty requires an understanding of the SRA's Assessment of Character and Suitability Rules, which requires disclosure of criminal conduct (at rule 3.1) and other conduct and behaviour (at rule 4.1). Below are extracts from these Rules,[5] which shows the breadth of notifiable matters.

Table 1: Criminal conduct. Source: SRA.

Most serious (A finding in this category is likely to result in refusal)	**Serious (A finding in this category may result in refusal)**
You have been convicted by a court of a criminal offence: • For which you received a custodial or suspended sentence; • Involving dishonesty, fraud, perjury, and/or bribery; • Of a violent or sexual nature; • Associated with obstructing the course of justice; • Which demonstrated behaviour showing signs of discrimination towards others; or • Associated with terrorism. You have been convicted by a court of more than one criminal offence (these could be less serious offences when considered in isolation but taken more seriously because of frequency and/or repetition). You have shown a pattern of criminal offences or criminal behaviours (e.g., starting from a caution but moving through to convictions). You have accepted a caution from the police for an offence involving dishonesty, violence or discrimination, or a sexual offence. You have been included on the Violent and Sex Offenders register.	You have accepted a caution for, or been convicted by a court of, a criminal offence not falling within the most serious category (which is likely to result in refusal). You are currently subject to a conditional discharge or bind over by a court.

Table 2: Other conduct and behaviour. Source: SRA.

Type of behaviour	Examples
Integrity and independence	You have behaved in a way: • Which is dishonest; • Which is violent; • Which is threatening or harassing; • Where there is evidence of discrimination towards others. You have misused your position to obtain pecuniary advantage. You have misused your position of trust in relation to vulnerable people. The SRA has evidence reflecting on the honesty and integrity of a person you are related to, affiliated with, or act together with where the SRA has reason to believe that the person may have an influence over the way in which you will exercise your authorised role.
Assessment offences	You have committed and/or have been adjudged by an education establishment to have committed a deliberate assessment offence, which amounts to plagiarism or cheating, in order to gain an advantage for you or others.
Financial conduct/ events	There is evidence: • That you have deliberately sought to avoid responsibility for your debts; • Of dishonesty in relation to the management of your finances; • That you have been declared bankrupt, entered into any individual voluntary arrangements, have a current County Court Judgment issued against you or have been made subject to a Debt Relief Order; • That any company, LLP or partnership of which you are/were a manager or owner has been the subject of a winding up order, an administrative order or an administrative receivership, or has otherwise been wound up or put into administration in circumstances of insolvency; • That you cannot satisfactorily manage your finances (e.g., you have fallen behind with six or more consecutive payments and/or have been registered with a credit reference agency); • That you are subject to possession proceedings (e.g., for falling behind on mortgage payments) and/or are subject to a Liability Order (e.g., for non-payment of council tax).
Regulatory or disciplinary findings	You have been made the subject of a serious disciplinary or regulatory finding, sanction, or action by a regulatory body and/or any court or other body hearing appeals in relation to disciplinary or regulatory findings. You have failed to disclose information to a regulatory body (including the SRA) when required to do so or have provided false or misleading information. You have significantly breached the requirements of a regulatory body. You have failed to comply with the reasonable requests of a regulatory body resulting in a finding against you. You have been rebuked, reprimanded, or received a warning about your conduct by a regulatory body. You are disqualified from being a charity trustee or a trustee for a charity under section 178(1) of the Charities Act 2011. You have been removed and/or disqualified as a company director.[6] You are a corporate person and other matters that call into question your fitness and propriety are disclosed or come to light. You have committed an offence under the Companies Acts.[7]

Points to make about this disclosure duty are as follows:

- The tables provided by the SRA (as shown above) are non-exhaustive and a role-holder with any concerns about behaviour that may be reportable should discuss this with the SRA.
- For example, the SRA is increasingly looking at "fitness to practice" issues and any health-related considerations that might have an impact on an individual's suitability. In this regard, the SRA is seeking to add to these Rules with wording to require that individuals with health issues are required to make these known to the SRA. Such changes must be approved by the LSB but the proposals are indicative of the SRA's thinking about matters which should be reportable.[8]
- The disclosure does not automatically mean that approval will be withdrawn. You are updating information already provided to the SRA so that it can fulfil its risk management responsibilities and ensure that nothing about the original approval decision should be re-evaluated.
- The disclosure must be made promptly and, whilst this term is not defined further by the SRA, it will be an aggravating feature in any subsequent investigation if the SRA considers that the individual delayed updating the SRA.
- The SRA lists aggravating and mitigating factors when evaluating new information. Aggravating factors include any of the following circumstances:
    - No evidence of successful rehabilitation;
    - No evidence of steps taken to remedy conduct;
    - No (or little) evidence of remorse;
    - Repeated behaviour, or a pattern of behaviour, or event occurred very recently;
    - The individual was in a position of trust;
    - The individual held a senior position;
    - The vulnerability of those impacted by the behaviour; or
    - The behaviour is likely to harm public confidence in the profession.

Mitigating factors include any of the following circumstances:

- Evidence of successful rehabilitation;
- Evidence of steps taken to remedy conduct;
- Evidence of remorse;
- A one-off event, or an event that occurred some time ago;
- The individual was in a junior or non-legal role;
- There is no evidence of harm being caused to individuals;
- The behaviour is unlikely to harm public confidence in the profession; or
- The availability of credible and cogent supporting references.

Withdrawal of approval

The approval and deemed approved process can be reversed. The SRA has the power to withdraw approval granted to a compliance officer under Rule 13.9 of the SRA Authorisation of Firms Rules. This power will be used if the SRA "*is not satisfied that the person is fit and proper to undertake the designated role*".

Examples of when withdrawal may be appropriate include:

- Where a newly disclosed character and suitability issue means that the role-holder is no longer deemed to have suitable attributes.
- Where the SRA becomes aware of an existing character and suitability issue that had not been properly disclosed to it during the original approval process.
- Where supervisory and enforcement action against the individual and/or the authorised law firm reveals non-compliance with regulatory requirements.

Temporary emergency approval of a COLP or COFA

We have already emphasised the need for pre-planning to ensure that there is no disruption to the maintenance of compliance officer roles within the authorised law firm. This is important as having a COLP and COFA is an authorisation condition.

However, the SRA acknowledges that there may be exceptional circumstances in which a COLP or COFA role-holder may be lost (usually because of unexpected death or sudden illness etc.), and the SRA Authorisation of Firms Rules contains a procedure for the temporary emergency approval of a compliance officer. This is stated at Rule 15. The SRA is explicit about the need for this procedure to be confined to genuine emergency scenarios.

In guidance to support understanding (Approval of role holders – 12 March 2021), we are given the following warning about the availability of this procedure:

> *"We will only grant the temporary approval if (rule 15.3 of the Authorisation of Firms Rules):*
> 1. *We are satisfied that you could not reasonably have started the application for approval in advance of the previous compliance officer ceasing to hold the role, and*
> 2. *On the face of the application and any other information immediately before us, there is no evidence suggesting that the new compliance officer is not fit and proper to be a compliance officer."*

The compliance steps that must be followed are as follows:

- The firm can apply for temporary approval under Rule 15 of the SRA Authorisation of Firms Rules only if an application is made within seven days of the existing approved COLP or COFA ceasing to hold the role.
- Temporary approval is granted if the SRA is satisfied that the circumstances were unforeseen and that there is nothing to suggest that the replacement COLP or COFA is not fit and proper.
- The replacement must consent to their designation.
- The replacement must not be disqualified.
- If stepping up as COLP, the replacement must be an authorised person.
- A substantive application must be submitted within 28 days of the commencement of the temporary approval (noting that if temporary authorisation is approved, it will run from the date the previous compliance officer ceased to hold their role).

References

1 According to the SRA glossary, Manager means:
- The sole principal in a recognised sole practice;
- A member of a LLP;
- A director of a company;
- A partner in a partnership; or
- In relation to any other body, a member of its governing body.

2 According to the SRA glossary, an Employee means an individual who is:
- a) Engaged under a contract of service by a person, firm or organisation or its wholly owned service company;
- b) Engaged under a contract for services, made between a firm or organisation and: That individual;
  1. An employment agency; or
  2. A company which is not held out to the public as providing legal services and is wholly owned and directed by that individual, or
  3. under which the person, firm or organisation has exclusive control over the individual's time for all or part of the individual's working week, save that:
     1. For the purposes of the SRA Financial Services (Scope) Rules, means an individual who is employed in connection with the firm's regulated financial services activities under a contract of service or under a contract for services such that he or she is held out as an employee or consultant of the firm
     2. For the purposes of the SRA Indemnity Insurance Rules and the MTC, means any person other than a principal:
        1. Employed or otherwise engaged in the insured firm's practice (including under a contract for services) including, without limitation, as a solicitor, lawyer, trainee solicitor or trainee lawyer, consultant, associate, locum tenens, agent, appointed person, office or clerical staff member or otherwise;
        2. Seconded to work in the insured firm's practice; or
        3. Seconded by the insured firm to work elsewhere,

        but does not include any person who is engaged by the insured firm under a contract for services in respect of any work where that person is required, whether under the SRA Indemnity Insurance Rules or under the rules of any other professional body, to take out or to be insured under separate professional indemnity insurance in respect of that work

     and the term "employer" is to be construed accordingly.

3 According to the SRA glossary, Authorised body means:
- A body that has been authorised by the SRA to practise as a licensed body or a recognised body; or
- A sole practitioner's practice that has been authorised by the SRA as a recognised sole practice.

4 According to the SRA glossary, Approved regulator means any body listed as an approved regulator in paragraph 1 of Schedule 4 to the LSA or designated as an approved regulator by an order under paragraph 17 of that Schedule.

5 Reproduced from the SRA Authorisation Rules with permission from the SRA, www.sra.org.uk.

6 According to the SRA glossary, Director means a director of a company; and in relation to a *societas Europaea* includes:

- In a two-tier system, a member of the management organ and a member of the supervisory organ; and
- In a one-tier system, a member of the administrative organ.

7 Companies Act 1985 and Companies Act 2006.

8 See SRA Consultation, March 2022: Rule changes on Health and Wellbeing, www.sra.org.uk/sra/consultations/consultation-listing/health-wellbeing-profession/?s=c.

Chapter 2:
Appointing your COLP and COFA

In chapter one, we considered how these roles evolved and the authorisation requirements associated with the roles. In this chapter we consider what the SRA requires from the role-holders by delving deeper into the source materials in the SRA Standards and Regulations. We also look at the attributes of the successful COLP and COFA, and the resources that are needed to ensure that there is a successful and purposeful relationship with managers and employees within the firm and also outside of the firm with the SRA.

Key extracts from STaRs

The responsibilities of the firm's compliance officers are stated in chapter nine of the SRA Code of Conduct for Firms. This is a sensible location for this information, bearing in mind that this Code of Conduct describes the standards and business controls that the SRA demands of all law firms that it has authorised to provide legal services to the public. The purpose of the Code of Conduct for Firms is to create and maintain the right culture and environment for the delivery of competent and ethical legal services to clients.

Paragraph 9.1 is addressed to the COLP:

"9.1 *If you are a COLP you must take all reasonable steps to:*

a) Ensure compliance with the terms and conditions of your firm's authorisation;

b) Ensure compliance by your firm and its managers, employees, or interest holders[1] *with the SRA's regulatory arrangements which apply to them;*

c) Ensure that your firm's managers and interest holders and those they employ or contract with do not cause or substantially contribute to a breach of the SRA's regulatory arrangements;

d) Ensure that a prompt report is made to the SRA of any facts or matters that you reasonably believe are capable of amounting to a serious breach of the terms and conditions of your firm's authorisation, or the SRA's regulatory arrangements which apply to your firm, managers, or employees;

e) Notwithstanding sub-paragraph (d), you ensure that the SRA is informed promptly of any facts or matters that you reasonably believe should be brought to its attention in order that it may investigate whether a serious breach of its regulatory arrangements has occurred or otherwise exercise its regulatory powers,

Save in relation to the matters which are the responsibility of the COFA as set out in paragraph 9.2 below."

Paragraph 9.2 is addressed to the COFA:

"*9.2 If you are a COFA, you must take all reasonable steps to:*

(a) Ensure that your firm and its managers and employees comply with any obligations imposed upon them under the SRA Accounts Rules;

(b) Ensure that a prompt report is made to the SRA of any facts or matters that you reasonably believe are capable of amounting to a serious breach of the SRA Accounts Rules which apply to them;

(c) Notwithstanding sub-paragraph (b), you ensure that the SRA is informed promptly of any facts or matters that you reasonably believe should be brought to its attention in order that it may investigate whether a serious breach of its regulatory arrangements has occurred or otherwise exercise its regulatory powers."

References to the "regulatory arrangements" are scattered throughout chapter nine. The meaning of this phrase is found in section 21 of the Legal Services Act 2007 and is by necessity extensive and means the SRA's arrangements in the following areas:

- Its arrangements for authorising persons to carry on reserved legal activities;
- Its arrangements (if any) for authorising persons to provide immigration advice or immigration services;
- Its practice rules;
- Its conduct rules;
- Its disciplinary arrangements in relation to regulated persons (including its discipline rules);

- Its qualification regulations;
- Its indemnification arrangements;
- Its compensation arrangements;
- Any other rules or regulations that apply to its regulatory relationship with regulated persons; and
- Its licensing rules.

The SRA currently sets outs its regulatory arrangements in the SRA Standards and Regulations (the STaRs).[2] The SRA describes the STaRs as "*the standards and requirements we expect our regulated community to achieve and observe, for the benefit of the clients they serve and in the public interest*".

Understanding this backdrop, and more generally the emphasis of the LSA, means that it is clear that the COLP's responsibilities in connection with regulatory arrangements is extensive. The only specific carve-out from the STaRs of benefit to the COLP is the SRA Accounts Rules, which fall within the COFA's jurisdiction. All other parts are either definitely or potentially within the COLP's remit. It is essential that the firm's COLP has considered the STaRs, and evaluated which parts are relevant because of the firm's circumstances and is satisfied with the compliance and business systems that the firm has put in place to manage behaviours and response.

The COFA's responsibilities are more specifically centred on the SRA Accounts Rules so, in more general terms, the role-holder is considering the correct handling and proper protection of client money. By implication, although not stated explicitly, the risk of mismanagement of client money will require the COFA to be satisfied about other financial topics, such as understanding the use and controls relating to the firm's business accounts and its own monies and also in respect of business viability and financial stability issues.

Compliance officer responsibilities are described separately from the firmwide responsibilities in respect of compliance and business systems and the expectations about managerial responsibilities. Very little should be read into this; the COLP and the COFA must be confident that how the law firm is run and managed supports their personal relationship with the SRA, and that managers understand how they are expected to behave and the role they have in respect of compliance.

Case study

In 2020, the Solicitors Disciplinary Tribunal decided to strike off the roll an experienced solicitor and sole principal for what were described as failings to "execute her role as steward of client monies with any diligence". In a separate, but related, ruling the firm's COFA admitted "manifest incompetence". The COFA was not a lawyer and said in his mitigation that he had "no experience" of the role before taking it on. The SDT found that "he had underestimated the role and did not fully comprehend the difficulties and challenges associated with accounting procedures". Because of his failings, the authorised law firm operated in serious breach of the Accounts Rules and client money was at risk. The COFA was made subject to an order banning him from working in SRA-authorised law firms without the regulator's permission and was ordered to pay costs of £2,500. The law firm was subject to an SRA intervention and closed down.

Compliance and business systems

The LSA has made it necessary for the SRA to take far more interest in the internal operations of law firms than had been the case for its predecessor regulatory body, the Law Society of England and Wales.

The STaRs deal with this through the inclusion of duties relating to compliance and business systems in chapter two of the SRA Code of Conduct for Firms, which states as follows:

"2.1 *You have effective governance structures, arrangements, systems and controls in place that ensure:*
- *(a) You comply with all the SRA's regulatory arrangements, as well as with other regulatory and legislative requirements, which apply to you;*
- *(b) Your managers and employees comply with the SRA's regulatory arrangements which apply to them;*
- *(c) Your managers and interest holders and those you employ or contract with do not cause or substantially contribute to a breach of the SRA's regulatory arrangements by you or your managers or employees;*
- *(d) Your compliance officers are able to discharge their duties under paragraphs 9.1 and 9.2 below.*

2.2 *You keep and maintain records to demonstrate compliance with your obligations under the SRA's regulatory arrangements.*

2.3 *You remain accountable for compliance with the SRA's regulatory arrangements where your work is carried out through others, including your managers and those you employ or contract with.*

2.4 *You actively monitor your financial stability and business viability. Once you are aware that you will cease to operate, you effect the orderly wind-down of your activities.*

2.5 *You identify, monitor and manage all material risks to your business, including those which may arise from your connected practices.*"[3]

Some pertinent points to extract from these statements are as follows:

- These requirements are not specifically or exclusively addressed to the compliance officers. This is deliberate and ties in with chapter eight of the same Code, which speaks to the firm's managers (see below). In fact, the direction in paragraph 2.1 (d) needs to be understood by the managers and owners of the law firm; its compliance and business systems must be effective in enabling the compliance officers to fulfil their personal duties and to be open and accountable to the SRA.
- The key method by which the COLP and COFA will fulfil their personal accountability commitments and be in a position to know when to notify the SRA of serious breaches of regulatory arrangements, is through the firm's maintenance of accurate records. This is described in paragraph 2.2. In additional guidance issued by the SRA to support compliance officers,[4] the SRA sets out its expectations about how this duty will be met: "*Your firm has an obligation to keep and maintain records to demonstrate compliance with its obligations. We therefore expect compliance officers to keep a record of all breaches that occur. These records are a key tool for you in understanding the risks to your business. They should help you to identify where things have gone wrong and whether there are any systemic problems inherent to your firm's processes.*"
- This guidance also steers us towards what the SRA expects to see in respect of the relationship between the compliance officers and the wider business: "*All firms need to decide how the COLP and COFA operate within their business structure. This involves making sure systems are in place to allow your firm to operate effectively and in compliance with the Standards and Regulations. In larger firms, or where the COLP and COFA are employees, as well as the right governance, the compliance officers must have clear reporting lines that empower them sufficiently to fulfil their roles. This is to make sure the COLP and COFA are able to implement changes or introduce new procedures to ensure compliance and good risk-management.*"

- It is important to understand the significance of the language used by the SRA and to respond accordingly. For example, we are told that governance structures and other arrangements must be "effective". This is a significant adjective in this context. In other words, your internal compliance and business systems must be successful in producing the intended result, which is that you respond appropriately to the regulatory arrangements. This description and expectation means that the SRA offers no prescriptive steer as to the composition of each individual law firm's systems of governance. Bear in mind, the SRA authorises over 10,000 entities. The arrangements that are appropriate for a sole practitioner who is his or her own COLP and COFA will be different to what might be considered suitable in different, larger practices. It is expected that each firm will consider its own needs and respond to the Code in an apt way. Whilst some people may find this frustrating and unhelpful, it should be stated that the role of the approved regulator does not dictate that it is required to be overtly helpful and also that the vagueness is necessary bearing in mind the requirement to accommodate a range of business models under one set of requirements.
- Similarly, the reference to the management of risk is both telling and vague. The SRA is a risk-based regulator (described in more detail in chapter three). It considers risks that may be present and that might jeopardise its own position as an approved regulator required to protect public interests and similar. In turn, it expects authorised law firms to contribute to risk management by identifying which risks are present in its environment and putting in place appropriate measures to monitor and mitigate such specified risks. This will be a judgement call.

The duties of managers in SRA authorised firms

The SRA applies the term "manager" to the following categories of individuals:

- "*The sole principal in a recognised sole practice;*
- *A member of an LLP;*
- *A director of a company;*
- *A partner in a partnership; or*
- *In relation to any other body, a member of its governing body.*"[5]

Paragraph 8.1 of the SRA Code of Conduct for Firms is addressed specifically to these individuals:

> *"If you are a manager, you are responsible for compliance by your firm with this Code. This responsibility is joint and several if you share management responsibility with other managers of the firm."*

This is an important statement, making several important points that must be understood if the firm is to have a satisfactory relationship with the SRA:

- Whilst the COLP and COFA have a defined and direct relationship with the SRA, and there are personal consequences if they default on their obligations, this does not absolve the law firm's managers from having responsibilities in respect of compliance. They are responsible for compliance regardless of their compliance in practice roles. This means that the effective governance response should be inclusive so that all managers are, at the very least, aware of compliance measures, intelligence from records kept etc., and so that there is confidence that compliance leadership comes from this senior cohort.
- It is not expected that managers would be able to override decisions made by compliance officers. In fact, any manager found to be behaving in such a way is likely to be investigated for misconduct issues.
- It is expected that all managers will understand their role in compliance, and as a consequence be able to promote an appropriate compliance culture of their business.

In other words, compliance officers do have a recognised role in their business' relationship but nothing in the language of the regulatory arrangements suggests that these individuals have sole responsibility for compliance. The response is expected to be one where collective responsibility is in evidence.

Compliance officers – necessary skills, knowledge, experience

It should be evident that considering who is suitable to be asked to volunteer for these roles (noting that it is a regulatory requirement that the role holders give their consent) is a significant matter. These are not token appointments and, if undertaken properly, require particular skillsets and characteristics to be displayed and used.

In many instances, there will be natural candidates for the roles. They will almost be self-selecting in that they are individuals who have had the necessary management and compliance experience.

Overall, a successful compliance officer – both in terms of delivering information to the SRA as expected and also with regard to their internal position and responsibilities – should have management experience and experience of implementing systems and procedures and managing risks to compliance. Whilst we have seen that these duties are described in chapter two of the SRA Code of Conduct for Firms (compliance and business systems) without explicit ownership stated to be with the COLP and COFA, in practice these will be within the compliance officers' job descriptions because there will be an element in self-interest in ensuring that what is put in place as governance structures is effective.

The compliance officers will also need to be familiar with the SRA Standards and Regulations. If they do not have this knowledge then it is unlikely that they will find their responsibilities manageable and, if approval is necessary rather than is deemed, it is unlikely that the SRA will consider them to be suitable candidates. There are many courses that are available to prospective compliance officers which will, firstly, help prospective officers decide whether they wish to volunteer and, secondly, provide necessary information about the knowledge needed.

In addition to this, there are other skills and attributes that are needed if the role and the role-holder are to be a good fit. We have seen that leadership skills coupled with a recognised seniority of position are advisable. This is recommended for a number of reasons, including:

- The SRA will expect to see compliance in practice. It will want evidence that systems and procedures are followed. This is more easily achievable if compliance is led by a senior member of the firm.
- The COLP and COFA must communicate to all managers and employees, and deliver compliance messages with authority so that reluctant colleagues understand that they have no choice but to comply.
- The COLP and COFA may need to make the ultimate unpopular decisions and make reports to the SRA of serious breaches of regulatory standards by both individuals within the firm (including other senior colleagues) and in respect of the business itself. They cannot allow themselves to be dissuaded from making a report and may need to forcefully and directly explain to colleagues why this is necessary.

- In some cases, the COLP and COFA's starting position may be with systems, controls, and attitudes that are not appropriate. They will need to persuade the business that a change of culture is necessary. These may be difficult messages, made harder if the COLP or COFA are not senior people themselves.

Good people skills are also important attributes. The COLP and the COFA must secure managers' and employees' interest and support in their topics so that everyone in the firm is on board in terms of understanding the importance of the correct compliance culture and the benefits that it will bring the firm. Most importantly, they should start with the manager layer of the firm; these senior colleagues are essential ambassadors and investors in the compliance regime. Without being able to achieve buy-in at this level, it will inevitably be an uphill struggle to get anyone else in the business to take compliance seriously.

The ability to persuade, inspire, enthuse, and even dictate in some situations, will create an atmosphere where compliance changes are more likely to happen and to become embedded in the firm's ethos. A compliance officer with an overly abrasive personality is unlikely, therefore, to be an appropriate role-holder as they may only succeed in making colleagues antagonistic and resilient to what are essentially necessary and sensible changes.

Given the messages and the information which a compliance officer will need to share both with colleagues and with the SRA, an ability to communicate effectively and persuasively will be an essential attribute.

Compliance officers – time factors and other considerations

Another consideration that must be factored into the prospective compliance officer's decision as to whether to consent to their appointment is whether the individual has the time to devote to this role, particularly if they fulfil another "day job" within the firm.

It is clear that the SRA sees these as key roles in improving and maintaining regulatory and professional standards in authorised law firms, rather than a minor role that is bolted on to other responsibilities and performed when time permits. There is also a level of personal responsibility attached to the role, meaning that it would be unwise of a role-holder, and unfair of the business' mangers, to ask someone to become a COLP or COFA if they do not have the time to dedicate to these duties. Although aspects of the role can be successfully delegated to others (for example, some firms have discrete teams fulfilling risk management and compliance functions), the COLP and COFA will always retain ultimate control for the compliance interaction with the SRA.

Therefore, whilst a firm's managing partner or senior partner may seem the obvious choice, this individual may not have the time to dedicate to compliance work. In many firms, the COLP and COFA roles sit alongside roles that have responsibility for strategic management and business development in perhaps a senior managerial triumvirate or executive board. In other firms, increasingly those firms with a more commercial practice or a global framework, the COLP role in particular is delegated to the firm's general counsel or to a senior colleague who works alongside the GC.

Some firms might consider that their practice manager, head of finance, or similar, is a suitable candidate to fulfil the COFA role. Many practice managers have made excellent COFAs but thought needs to be given as to whether the individual has sufficient presence in the business, is of senior standing, whether they have knowledge of all necessary aspects of regulation and the role of the SRA and the STaRs, and whether they have the experience of strategic thinking that is necessary.

Specific considerations about the COFA role

As hinted at in the preceding paragraph, there may be particular difficulties in appointing a suitably experienced individual to the COFA role. Unlike the COLP, a COFA does not have to be a lawyer. It is not always an easy fit to find someone who not only has the appropriately detailed knowledge of accounting and book-keeping skills but also knows enough about the SRA regulatory arrangements and the exact requirements of the SRA Accounts Rules and the overlap with other topics of regulatory concern.

Whilst those involved with handling client money on a daily basis, such as employees working in the finance or accounts team, might seem a sensible choice on one level, they may not have sufficient seniority or experience to be at ease in dealing with the management team and senior lawyers or have the confidence to instigate changes to systems and culture.

The finance director, or similar, may also be someone who may be a likely prospect. The key concerns with their suitability will be whether they have the time to have proper and thorough oversight of the firm's accounting systems and whether they have the necessary knowledge of the SRA Accounts Rules given that their main focus might be on the firm's own financial position. If there is a gap in knowledge of this type, then this can be remedied by an intensive training programme on the Accounts Rules and their practical application to the protection and holding of client money. This is recommended; without evidence of detailed knowledge of the Accounts Rules, the SRA is unlikely to approve an individual as a COFA.

Alternatively, there is no reason why a solicitor or other lawyer could not be the firm's COFA. Here, however, the learning curve is likely to require the acquisition of the detailed knowledge of book-keeping that will enable the role-holder to satisfy themselves on accounting matters. There would also be a need to have a thorough working knowledge of the SRA Accounts Rules, which might justify refresher training on this topic.

Can the COLP and COFA be the same person?

One option that some firms favour – and a course of action which by necessity a recognised sole practitioner is likely to adopt – is that of having one individual responsible for both the COLP and COFA roles.

This is not a decision to be taken lightly given what is involved in each of these tasks and time considerations. However, there may be some logic in pursuing this option, particularly if the role-holder does not have any fee earning responsibilities and does have a background in risk management and compliance. Of course, this does mean that the combined roles must be held by a solicitor or other qualified lawyer (because of the requirements of the COLP role).

The advantages of this approach are these:

- One person will have sole responsibility for the firm's compliance arrangements, which will give absolute clarity as to who is in control of all aspects of compliance.
- The management team will be dealing with one rather than two people in terms of objective setting, reports etc.
- One person will have control of all the reporting obligations, thereby reducing the risk of failure to report because of a lack of clear ownership.
- Consistent decision-making about the nature of serious (and therefore reportable) breaches because this is the responsibility of one person.
- All communications with the SRA, and to all managers and employees, will be channelled through one individual who will have a complete overview of the SRA requirements.

Certain disadvantages must be borne in mind:

- Lack of support from someone with comparable responsibilities; being both COLP and COFA could be a solitary role with no one in a comparable position with which to discuss concerns etc.
- Less cover for holidays, illness or other absences, or simply to deal with busy periods.
- Lack of discussion about regulatory matters might hinder justified decision-making.

Where there are choices about the numbers of compliance officers, then in making a decision, much will depend on the potential benefits to the firm and the willingness of a chosen individual to undertake both roles.

Can we buy in a COLP or COFA?

We have already discussed the requirement for the compliance officer roles to be filled by a manager or employee which satisfy the SRA definitions of these terms.

With this as the regulatory starting point, there is always the option to buy in the skills needed through the hiring of a new member of staff where there are no obvious internal candidates or no one willing to volunteer to take these roles on. This can be beneficial; someone joining the firm who has not grown up with the existing systems and controls may well have a fresh perspective for what is needed and for spotting risks that familiarity may have led longstanding members of the firm to overlook. It may also be easier for "fresh blood" to make changes as they do not have allegiances within the firm, which might constrain an internal candidate.

References

1 According to the SRA glossary, an Interest holder means a person who has an interest or an indirect interest, or holds a material interest, in a body (and "indirect interest" and "interest" have the same meaning as in the LSA), and references to "holds an interest" shall be construed accordingly.

2 www.sra.org.uk/solicitors/standards-regulations/

3 According to the SRA glossary, Connected practices means a body providing legal services, established outside England and Wales which is not an overseas practice or an excluded body but is otherwise connected to an authorised body in England and Wales, by virtue of:

a. being a parent undertaking, within the meaning of section 1162 of the Companies Act 2006, of the authorised body;
b. being jointly managed or owned, or having a partner, member or owner in common, or controlled by or, with the authorised body;
c. participating in a joint enterprise or across its practice generally, sharing costs, revenue or profits related to the provision of legal services with the authorised body; or
d. common branding,

and in this definition:

1. a "body" means a natural person or company, LLP or partnership or other body corporate or unincorporated association or business entity; and
2. an "excluded body" means a body which is part of:
    1. a Verein or similar group structure involving more than one body providing legal services in respect of which the authorised body in England and Wales connected to it is not regarded as being the body which is the headquarters of that Verein or similar group structure or a significant part of it;
    2. a joint practice, alliance or association or association with the authorised body in England and Wales connected to it which is controlled by a body providing legal services outside England and Wales; or
    3. a group of affiliated bodies providing legal services which is not managed or controlled by an authorised body in England and Wales
3. A "joint enterprise" means any contractual arrangements between two or more independent bodies which provide legal services, for profit and/or other defined purpose or goal which apply generally between them, not just agreed on a matter by matter basis
4. "Common branding" means the use of a name, term, design, symbol, words or a combination of these that identifies two or more legal practices as distinct from other legal practices or an express statement that a legal practice is practising in association with one or more other named firms.

4 www.sra.org.uk/solicitors/guidance/responsibilities-of-colps-and-cofas/

5 www.sra.org.uk/solicitors/standards-regulations/glossary/#manager

Chapter 3: SRA – understanding entity and risk-based regulation

We have discussed the recent history of regulation of the legal services market in England and Wales and introduced the compliance officer regime and thought about how COLPs and COFAs should be chosen and what attributes they should possess. In this chapter we look at the changes from the SRA's perspective and how this has an effect on the COLP and COFA and their relationship with the SRA. Information such as this supports compliance officers to make informed decisions about internal risk management and when needing to persuade colleagues about compliance duties, and in connection with external communications with the SRA.

Regulatory objectives and a changed approach to regulation

The Legal Services Act 2007 (the LSA) and the Legal Services Board (the LSB) have caused the SRA to have a very different regulatory approach to that of its predecessor, the Law Society of England and Wales. It is a proactive regulator and bases its work and priorities on risk-based analysis of the impact of behaviours of those individuals that it authorises and that which it authorises. It is also styled as a proportionate regulator, taking into consideration the risks posed by behaviours and responding accordingly. Integral to this approach is the need for a more open and cooperative relationship between the SRA and those it regulates. This is a two-way process, and the behaviours of the COLP and the COFA will be key to its success.

The impact of the LSA on the work of approved regulators

One of the main changes enabled by the language of the LSA has been the adoption of a set of regulatory objectives for approved regulators. Sir David Clementi, whose report to the UK government in 2004 on the state of legal services provision[1] led to the LSA, identified that the lack of any regulatory objectives was a failing that meant there was a lack of clarity about the role of regulation and a consequent lack of consistency amongst the various regulatory bodies.

The advocates of regulation explain that it provides a necessary framework within which standards are set so that the public interest is protected. Regulation promotes consistency, allays concerns about the harm to consumers that may arise if certain services or functions are unregulated, prevents the provision of services that cut regulatory corners, and provides a system of supervision and enforcement to deal with behaviours that fall below an accepted and industry-wide standard.

Section 1 of the LSA created the regulatory boundaries that had been identified as missing. The gap was filled with "regulatory objectives" and "professional principles" that approved regulators must use to justify their work, and which the LSB uses to test the effectiveness of the approved regulators.

The eight regulatory objectives are:

1. Protecting and promoting the public interest;
2. Supporting the constitutional principle of the rule of law;
3. Improving access to justice;
4. Protecting and promoting the interests of consumers;
5. Promoting competition in the provision of services within subsection (2);
6. Encouraging an independent, strong, diverse, and effective legal profession;
7. Increasing public understanding of the citizen's legal rights and duties; and
8. Promoting and maintaining adherence to the professional principles.

The professional principles are described in section 1(3) of the LSA and are directed at "authorised persons" who are told:

1. That authorised persons should act with independence and integrity;
2. That authorised persons should maintain proper standards of work;
3. That authorised persons should act in the best interests of their clients;
4. That persons who exercise before any court a right of audience, or conduct litigation in relation to proceedings in any court, by virtue of being authorised persons should comply with their duty to the court to act with independence in the interests of justice; and
5. That the affairs of clients should be kept confidential.

The LSB, as overarching regulator, has a statutory obligation to promote the objectives, and all approved regulators, including the SRA, have a duty to have regard to them in all their activities. In some cases, how this is put into practice will be obvious. For example, much of this wording will be familiar to anyone with knowledge of the SRA Standards and Regulations and many of the professional principles in the LSA have been translated into the SRA Principles and/or professional duties in the SRA Codes of Conduct.

The regulatory objectives have caused the SRA to focus its attention on how best to protect the public interest. It decided, bearing in mind its limited resources and statutory duties, that taking a risk-based approach is the most effective way of identifying and dealing with individuals and authorised law firms that potentially or actually present unacceptable levels of risk to their client and/or to the public at large. This formula is described as risk-based regulation.

The SRA's approach to risk

The SRA has rapidly developed its approach to risk and publishes a substantial amount of information about how it assesses and deals with risk. Primarily, the SRA sees risks in terms of risks to it, as a regulator, in meeting the regulatory objectives, and risks to consumers when authorised persons behave in a way that indirectly compromises the regulatory objectives or directly contravenes the professional principles.

It does not expect firms to operate in a zero-risk environment; this is unrealistic and not achievable. Instead, it expects firms to identify risks present in their environment (triggered by a consideration of services provided, to whom, and by whom etc.) and to have systems and procedures designed to manage and mitigate risk events. Firms are helped in understanding how risks are prioritised through the publication of risk materials by the SRA. These are all available from the SRA website and are essential reading for compliance officers as they provide indicators of SRA risk thinking. Two resources are particularly useful:

- SRA Risk Outlook[2] – this is an annual update of what the SRA regards as high risk and emerging risk circumstances. This contains an explanation of regulatory concern with, usually, pointers about what would constitute good and poor practice within law firms. Common themes are the protection of client money, anti-money laundering responses; integrity and ethics; diversity in the profession; and information and cyber security management. Lately, emerging themes have focused on the impact of the COVID-19 pandemic and the current state of the legal services market.

- SRA Update[3] – this is (usually, but not always) a monthly updater providing both general updates about SRA work and also with compliance updates.

The SRA's risk-based regulation, and how this manifests in the work undertaken by the SRA, is crucial knowledge for the COLP and COFA. It provides useful intelligence about issues that are likely to concern the SRA, and in this way it provides a useful steer as to internal priorities.

Information collected to assess risk

The SRA's expectation is that we (throughout this book "we" refers to solicitors and law firms) will gather and analyse information about how safely legal services are provided, and so that breaches can be recorded and serious breaches notified to the SRA with appropriate promptness.

Regulatory reach over the authorised law firm

One of the major compliance challenges for compliance officers and managers of the business is to ensure that everyone within the authorised business understands the scope of regulatory reach. Of course, the SRA has a direct regulatory reach with solicitors (and also Registered European and Registered Foreign lawyers) because these individual need current certification/registration in order to practise.

Significantly, this regulatory reach is extended through the authorised entity status, to all other managers and employees in this business. Clues about this are provided in the introduction to the Code in which the SRA states:

> *"A serious failure to meet our standards or a serious breach of our regulatory requirements may lead to our taking regulatory action against the firm itself as an entity, or its managers or compliance officers, who each have responsibilities for ensuring that the standards and requirements are met. We may also take action against employees working within the firm for any breaches for which they are responsible. A failure or breach may be serious either in isolation or because it comprises a persistent or concerning pattern of behaviour."*

Additional clarification of this point, and the effect of non-compliance by non-authorised individuals employed in the authorised entity, is in the

SRA guidance document, "How we regulate non-authorised persons".[4] Bear in mind the following commentary:

> *"This guidance aims to identify and explain how you are regulated by us and how we exercise our disciplinary and regulatory decision-making powers in respect of you. Our approach to making decisions about you is the same as for solicitors, RELs and RFLs. The public should be able to trust you in the delivery of legal services to act competently and ethically."*

The SRA's supervision and enforcement work

Supervision is the process by which the SRA identifies and evaluates risk in practice. It does this through an internal supervision department. Supervisory activities include random and targeted firm visits (either in person or virtually) and thematic reviews by which the SRA educates itself as to good and poor practice.

Investigation and enforcement

The SRA's investigation and enforcement teams have a wide range of options available to deal with individuals and authorised firms that present a risk to the regulatory objectives and/or adherence to the professional principles.

For example, it can ask for formal explanations, request or order the production of documents, and initiate forensic investigations of a firm's accounts. Where wrongdoing is found, appropriate disciplinary or administrative action can be taken. In the most serious cases, usually where dishonesty is involved, the matter will be referred to the Solicitors Disciplinary Tribunal[5] as this body has powers to suspend or strike individuals from practice and otherwise prevent them from being employed in authorised law firms.

Where there is immediate and severe risk to the client, usually in cases involving risks to client money, the SRA can exercise statutory powers to intervene in a law firm and close it down.

The SRA also has administrative powers that enable it to take control over individuals and firms, such as imposing conditions on a solicitor's practising certificate or disqualifying an individual from being a compliance officer, as we will see later in this chapter.

Case study

In 2021, the SDT agreed to intervention in a law firm because the solicitor-owner had failed to implement effective governance, compliance, and business systems such that his firm was described as a "complete shambles". Whilst the SDT did not question the individual's competencies in respect of legal knowledge, it was found that he did not have adequate skills to be a COLP, COFA, or a sole proprietor. The SDT decided that an intervention was necessary on the grounds of public interest and public protection.

What this style of regulation means for the COLP and the COFA

Cooperation, transparency, and openness are the watchwords of the SRA and define the relationship that the SRA assumes that it will enjoy with individuals and with authorised law firms. It is only by having access to all relevant information that the SRA can be an effective regulator and demonstrate that its work supports the regulatory objectives.

To do this, it needs the cooperation of authorised individuals and the firm to provide the necessary information. Most of the intelligence needed is expected to be provided by the COLP and the COFA (although it also expects prompt whistleblowing from others as and when necessary).

The information now required is more extensive than many members of the profession might feel comfortable with. It includes a duty to self-report about non-compliance with regulatory obligations and professional duties, disclosures about certain incidents that occur in individuals' private lives, and information about the financial stability and business viability of authorised law firms. Individuals and firms would be both foolish and reckless to hope that mistakes will go unnoticed. All mistakes must be evaluated, recorded and, in some cases, reported promptly to the SRA.

The SRA has repeatedly reassured firms that where there is cooperation, the SRA will take this into account when dealing with the issues that have arisen. In other words, openness and willingness to cooperate will be considered, subject, of course, to the overriding need to protect the public interest. With all this in mind, it is clear that it is not only in the interests of COLPs and COFAs, but also all owners and managers of their authorised law firms, that the firm develops a relationship of trust with the SRA so that the SRA has confidence that there will be openness about any issues that might affect their firms.

Enforcement powers against the COLP and COFA

We have already seen that the COLP and the COFA are required to consent to their roles; in other words, they are expected to be volunteers and not coerced into accepting these positions. This is partly because of the responsibilities attached to the role with the need to be a compliance-led player within the firm and the prime point of contact with the SRA.

Another reason why it is sensible for the role-holders to reflect on these positions before accepting any invitation is because of the personal consequences of non-compliance. If the SRA decides that a COLP or COFA has failed to fulfil their role properly, there are sanctions that can be imposed on the individual. These are:

- Conditions on approval of the role-holder;
- Revocation of approval;
- Disqualification from holding the role;
- Fines; and
- If a solicitor is a role-holder then suspension or striking-off and, if a non-solicitor, then an order made prohibiting their employment in an SRA-authorised law firm.

Case study

In 2016, a COFA was rebuked and fined £2,000 by the SRA for allowing their firm's bank account to be used as a banking facility. The COFA was an accountant and the firm's practice manager. In a regulatory settlement agreement with the SRA, the COFA admitted that he permitted banking services through the client account, allowed improper withdrawal and transfers, and had failed to meet his obligations as a compliance officer.

In mitigation, the COFA said he was not clear about the banking prohibition but that systems and controls had been amended to avoid repetition. His conduct was a result of "misunderstandings and unintended breaches".

In addition to the rebuke and fine, the COFA was also ordered to pay costs of £1,339.

The more severe of these sanctions are within the control of the Solicitors Disciplinary Tribunal, although it is interesting to note that, following a change in legislation in July 2022, the maximum fine the SRA can impose on solicitors and non-ABS firms (and individuals working in them) has been increased to £25,000.[6]

References

1 https://webarchive.nationalarchives.gov.uk/ukgwa/20070307120821/http:/www.legal-services-review.org.uk/content/consult/consult_reviewpaper.pdf
2 www.sra.org.uk/sra/research-publications/risk-outlook-202122/
3 www.sra.org.uk/sra/news/sra-update/
4 www.sra.org.uk/solicitors/guidance/general-regulation-non-authorised-persons/
5 www.solicitorstribunal.org.uk/
6 www.sra.org.uk/statement-fining-powers

Chapter 4:
The COLP's essential knowledge and suggested systems and controls

In this chapter we consider what knowledge the COLP must acquire, and with this understanding we then offer some suggestions for the implementation of well-designed systems and controls to ensure effective management of key topics. Of course, it is not intended that the COLP is the sole architect of the firm's compliance in practice tools, but they will certainly want to have an influential role in ensuring that these are fit for their own purpose. The COLP will not be able to make a judgement of this nature without first acquiring some essential knowledge about regulation and the SRA's regulatory manual, the SRA Standards and Regulations (the STaRs).

The extent of the COLP's responsibilities contrasted with the role of the COLP and the firm's managers

A reminder of the extent of the COLP's responsibilities, which will set the scene for their preparatory work before assuming the roles, will be gained by reading the general conditions of authorisation in rule 8 of the SRA Authorisation of Firms Rules.[1]

It is clear that compliance officers join others in the firm as being recognised as having important roles in the SRA's regime. For example, Rule 9 of the Authorisation of Firms Rules sets out requirements for the managers, owners, and compliance officers of the authorised firms under the heading "management, control, and supervision". These groups are viewed as the senior roles within the business occupying what the SRA describes as positions of responsibility and trust. It stands to reason that the regulator insists on having input in the composition of law firms as these are the vehicles through which legal services will be provided and managers, owners, and compliance officers are in positions of influence within the firms.

Added to the indicators in the Authorisation of Firms Rules is guidance that makes it clear that compliance responsibilities are shared. This guidance[2] includes the following statements:

- Managers have ultimate responsibility for how their firm is run. Specifically, the SRA says, they must make sure that it complies with all legislative and regulatory requirements, which means making sure that it has all the systems needed to achieve that objective.
- Owners can potentially exert significant influence over the law firm. The SRA cautions against any environment in which owners could do anything that causes the firm, or anyone in it, to breach their own regulatory obligations.
- Compliance officers have specific responsibility for ensuring that the firm, its managers, and employees comply with regulatory requirements. The guidance suggests that compliance officers are responsible for recording any breaches of the regulatory requirements. It has to be said that this is not as clearly stated in the SRA Code of Conduct for Firms but notwithstanding any inconsistency between the Rules and the guidance, it certainly is best practice for compliance officers to own this responsibility. This is because they are most definitely responsible for reporting breaches as necessary to the SRA and it would be difficult to do this properly without being confident that the underlying compliance records are being maintained.

The language of the Rules and the SRA guidance suggests a symbiotic relationship between the firm's and manager's duties, and those of the COLP and COFA. In fact, the ability of compliance officers to take the steps necessary to ensure compliance is dependent on managers promoting and supporting an appropriate environment.

This expectation is made clear in other parts of the SRA Code of Conduct for Firms. The introduction states:

> *"This Code of Conduct describes the standards and business controls that we, the SRA, and the public expect of firms (including sole practices) authorised by us to provide legal services. These aim to create and maintain the right culture and environment for the delivery of competent and ethical legal services to clients. These apply in the context of your practice: the way you run your business and all your professional activities."*

Paragraph 2.1 (c) of this Code talks to managers and demands that they have effective governance structures and similar that ensure *"your compliance officers are able to discharge their duties under paragraphs 9.1 and 9.2"*.

This message is not new. In fact, the SRA has been keen to provide reassurance to prospective compliance officers that they are not solely responsible for regulatory relationships since the very early days of this regime. For example, speaking at a risk management conference in 2011, a senior SRA executive made clear that COLPs cannot be wheeled out as convenient scapegoats if "something hits the fan". Controlling interests cannot hide behind their COLP – particularly if their COLP has been under-resourced without sufficient backing from the top. Ultimate responsibility and culpability for regulatory compliance with outcomes-focused regulation still lies with the most senior people, and the SRA will swiftly move in that direction, he warned at the time, if it detects serious unresolved issues.

Key knowledge from the SRA Standards and Regulations of relevance to the COLP

The subjects that concern the COLP are largely contained in the SRA Standards and Regulations (the STaRs), which is the SRA's current manual of rules and regulations that shape its regulatory regime. The STaRs manual has been in force since 25 November 2019. It is in fact the second manual produced by the SRA; its predecessor was the SRA Handbook,[3] which was launched in 2011 and facilitated a new style of regulation described as outcomes-focused regulation (OFR).

This was one of the more transformative responses to the Legal Services Act in that the Handbook was a move away from detailed, precise, and prescriptive rules to language that focused on objectives that must be achieved. This was particularly in evidence in the SRA Code of Conduct 2011, which contained outcomes that applied to professional conduct. The outcomes were mandatory behaviours that firms, and the individuals working within them, were expected to achieve in order to produce the right outcome for an individual client and in order to be seen to be achieving the underlying core values of ethical behaviour described in the SRA Principles, which pervaded all areas of practice.

This change of style was challenging for many solicitors and for the COLP with their responsibilities for managing compliance. Because the SRA no longer routinely tells us how to comply, this means that firms are placed in a position whereby they are expected to manage adaptations for themselves and both formulate and implement systems and controls.

The SRA Handbook proved to have been drafted in a format that needed constant update (by its last year of use, we were working with version 21). The STaRs were introduced as a replacement in 2019 and so far have been successful in one of their objectives in that there have been only minor amendments and no need to progress beyond the first version.

The language is less outcomes-focused and instead now describes rules, regulations, and duties that must be met. However, this is not a departure from outcomes-focused regulation, which is very much this regulator's preferred style, and it is still the position that we are given standards to achieve but left to consider our own best way of reaching a position of compliance. As importantly, this style of regulation, and the focus on achieving deliverable objectives, means that we are expected to justify our responses to various regulatory challenges.

Many firms decided that with the change of rulebook in 2019, it would be an appropriate moment to replace the COLP. In some firms, it has been the case that the original COLP decided to hand over the regulatory baton at that point. Other firms have had the same role-holder since the position went live in January 2013 and have continued into the STaRs era with the same role-holder.

Regardless of any of these factors, the SRA expected a smooth transition to the STaRs and there has been no period of grace in which to become accustomed to the new manual. We are expected to understand that the SRA's interest extends beyond individual behaviour to the culture of the environment in which it provides legal services. We are expected to understand that the interest intrudes into the firm's business psyche so that issues such as business viability are a regulatory concern, and we are expected to be able to demonstrate compliance in practice.

A well-equipped COLP will have a comprehensive knowledge of the STaRs so that those sections that are relevant to the COLP's reporting duties have been identified, discussed, and systems of controls (in the form of policies, procedures, audits, registers, and records) have been adopted that place the COLP in the position that they can both contribute to the firm's continuing success and also ensure that they are appropriately accountable to the SRA.

The COLP's homework must therefore include a review of the STaRs as the starting point.

Overview of the STaRs from the COLP's perspective

In layperson's language, the COLP will be concerned with matters that might impact the COLP's reporting duties to the SRA and these are broadly concerned with matters relating to managers' and employees' behaviours and the way in which services are offered to clients. Is there the proper professionalism on display?

The following paragraphs provide guidance on those sections of the STaRs that are in the COLP's domain. It is not a substitute for careful reading of the STaRs. However, it does provide an introduction on the focus of the content, and the main points of interest to the SRA, together with some suggestions about systems and controls that may be useful to demonstrate the required "effective governance" of the "regulatory arrangements" as mandated by the objectives in chapter two of the SRA Code of Conduct for Firms.[4]

SRA Principles

These are described by the SRA as "*the fundamental tenets of ethical behaviour that we, the SRA, expect of those that we regulate*". In other words, these are the core professional values or behaviours. These ought not to come as a surprise to solicitors, but the COLP will want to ensure that both solicitor-colleagues, plus all other managers and employees, understand their application. This is because the Principles are a collection of behaviours that apply to all members of the firm. This is regardless of qualification or role and can in some circumstances be applied to behaviours outside of practice (as described in chapter eight).

Where useful, policies and procedures are described below. However, because of the high-level and all-pervasive nature of the seven behaviours, these are concepts where compliance officers and managers of the firm lead by example and by creating the right culture in which professional behaviour is facilitated.

Ensuring these Principles are met requires an explanation of managers' expectations; asking the managers to lead by example; a workplace culture of openness and accountability rather than blame and shame; an understanding that what might be legal is not necessarily always ethical; an acknowledgement that ethical behaviour must never be compromised; awareness that mistakes will happen but what happens next is often more significant; and adequate knowledge of regulatory requirements facilitated through training and discussion.

Principle 1

"You act in a way that upholds the constitutional principle of the rule of law and the proper administration of justice."

The SRA interprets the reference to the rule of law as the principle that the law is of equal application. The reference to the proper administration of justice is an acknowledgement that a solicitor is an officer of the court and the court has jurisdictional powers over solicitors. This position means that the solicitor's duty to the court must, if a conflict arises, take precedence over other duties such as acting in a client's best interest.

In the case of *Arthur J S Hall v. Simons* (2002) 1 AC 615, we were told:

> *"Lawyers conducting litigation owe a divided loyalty. They have a duty to their clients, but they may not win by whatever means. They also owe a duty to the court and the administration of justice… Sometimes the performance of these duties to the court may annoy the client. So, it was said, the possibility of a claim for negligence might inhibit the lawyer from acting in accordance with his overriding duty to the court. That would be prejudicial to the interests of justice."*

Examples of breaches of Principle 1 include abuse of the judicial process; misleading the court; failing to comply with the lawful exercise of investigative powers (including failing to provide a specimen of breath to the police or failing to produce documents when lawfully sought by the SRA); involvement in or links to organised crime; and involvement in money laundering, amongst others.

Case study

In 2021, a solicitor who had previously been found by a High Court Judge to have deliberately misled the Court was subsequently struck off the roll of solicitors by the Solicitors Disciplinary Tribunal. The solicitor was found to have allowed leading counsel to make misleading submissions to the court and misleading the other side's legal team.

Systems and controls that should be considered to support effective governance include:

- Ensuring that all colleagues understand the significance of being able to demonstrate compliance with the law, both in respect of the services provided to clients and also in their personal lives;
- Supporting colleagues so that they do not compromise their personal position because of client or commercial pressures;
- Ensuring that the firm is well-run with appropriate strategic planning to ensure financial and business viability that supports ethical decision-making; and
- Support for all managers and employees to be open, accountable, and able to report notifiable matters.

Principle 2
"You act in a way that upholds public trust and confidence in the solicitors' profession and in legal services provided by authorised persons."

In the case of *Bolton v. Law Society* (1994) WLR 512, we were told, "*It is required of lawyers practicing in this country that they should discharge their professional duties with integrity, probity and complete trustworthiness*" and that the purpose of enforcement action against solicitors was in part "*to maintain the reputation of the solicitors' profession as one in which every member, of whatever standing, may be trusted to the ends of the earth*". Any behaviours that jeopardise the confidence that the public should have in the profession will result in disciplinary action and, usually, the severest of sanctions.

Examples of activities that are likely to compromise Principle 2 include criminal offences, offensive communications, taking advantage of clients and others because of that person's position or vulnerabilities, inappropriate use of non-disclosure agreements, and similar.

Case study
In 2022, a former partner in a law firm was suspended from practice for one year for accepting a cash gift of £2,500 from a client and asking that client to pay him an introduction fee in respect of a referral to a third party. Both acts were in breach of the law firm's internal policies and the partner had received training in respect of these. The Solicitors Disciplinary Tribunal considered that this behaviour "threatens the confidence and trust the public places in solicitors to handle their funds".

Systems and controls that should be considered to support effective governance include:

- Social media policy;
- Gifts policy;
- Anti-bribery and corruption policy;
- Policy in respect of expected behaviours outside of practice or when entertaining clients etc.; and
- Training of managers and HR staff about NDAs.

Principle 3

"You act with independence."

This behaviour applies both to individuals and the authorised firm as an entity. It describes the ability to give independent advice to clients as well as acts that compromise compliance with regulatory duties such as may be the case if a third party exerts control over an individual or a firm. Independence may also be compromised if a manager or employee exerts pressure on another colleague so that their behaviour is unprofessional as a consequence.

Case study

In 2022, the SRA rebuked a law firm for its conduct of a group action in circumstances where it was held that its independence had been compromised. The firm had been retained by a membership body to bring claims on behalf of almost 65,000 of its members in an action against British Airways. The case was struck out in the courts with Rose J finding that the law firm was acting for claimants that had not authorised the claim being brought in their names. The SRA found that the law firm mainly received instructions from the membership body's agent. The firm accepted that it had not made adequate enquiry and that its independence had been compromised by relying on a third party to verify which claimants were entitled to make a claim. In addition to the rebuke, the firm was also ordered to pay costs of almost £11,000.

Systems and controls that should be considered to support effective governance include:

- Scrutiny of referral arrangements with designated responsibilities for monitoring arrangements with third parties and communications with clients who may be impacted by these;
- Referrals and introductions policy; and
- Whistleblowing policy.

Principle 4
"You act with honesty."

In the case of *Wingate v. The SRA* and *Malines v. The SRA* (2018) EWCA Civ 366, Lord Justice Jackson said:

> *"Honesty is a basic moral quality which is expected of all members of society. It involves being truthful about important matters and respecting the property rights of others. Telling lies about things that matter or committing fraud or stealing are generally regarded as dishonest conduct... The legal concept of dishonesty is grounded upon the shared values of our multi-cultural society. Because dishonesty is grounded upon basic shared values, there is no undue difficulty in identifying what is or is not dishonest."*

Solicitors must be honest – they are officers of the court and must conduct cases in an honest manner and not misuse the court forum; they handle other people's money and assets; and they use their legal skills to resolve legal dilemmas and are trusted as a consequence with client information. Similar behaviours are expected of non-solicitors employed in authorised law firms.

A solicitor found to be dishonest is likely to be removed from the roll of solicitors. A non-solicitor employed in an authorised firm is likely to be made subject to an order so that they cannot be employed in an authorised firm except with SRA permission. Where there is suspected dishonesty by managers or employees in a law firm then the SRA may intervene in the firm and withdraw its authorised status.

The SRA applies a two-stage test when considering dishonest conduct, described in *Ivey v. Genting Casinos (UK) Limited t/a Crockfords* (2017) UKSC 67:

1. What was the individual's genuine knowledge or belief as to the facts at the time?
2. In view of their knowledge or belief at the time, was their conduct dishonest by the standards of ordinary decent people?

Some examples of disciplinary action that have been taken due to dishonest behaviour have included the following:

- Taking or using someone else's money without their knowledge or agreement even if the solicitor did not intend to permanently deprive the other person of that money;

- Lying to or misleading another a person;
- Knowingly bringing a false case to a court;
- Helping other people to act improperly such as with dubious investment schemes;
- Giving false information to their firm's insurer;
- Misleading a court, tribunal or a regulatory body;
- Lying on a CV; and
- Backdating or creating false documents.

Systems and controls that should be considered to support effective governance include:

- Training of managers and HR colleagues about recruitment policies and necessary screening;
- Ensuring that there is a reporting procedure that facilitates prompt disclosures; and
- Whistleblowing policy.

Principle 5
"You act with integrity."

Continuing the discussion about lessons learned from the *Wingate & Malins* case (see above), Lord Justice Jackson also stated:

> *"Integrity is a more nebulous concept… In professional codes of conduct, the term 'integrity' is a useful shorthand to express the higher standards which society expects from professional persons and which the professions expect from their own members… The underlying rationale is that the professions have a privileged and trusted role in society. In return they are required to live up to their own professional standards… Integrity connotes adherence to the ethical standards of one's own profession. That involves more than mere honesty."*

This Principle is wider than just acting dishonestly or, expressed another way, it is possible to behave without integrity without being dishonest. For example, the SRA says that it is likely to take disciplinary action on the grounds of a breach of Principle 5 in the following circumstances:

- Where there has been a wilful or reckless disregard of the STaRs or legal requirements, which would include an indifference to relevant provisions or consequences of a breach;
- Where there is evidence of taking unfair advantage of a client or a third party;
- Where there is knowing or reckless conduct, which has caused harm or distress to another; and
- Where clients or third parties have been misled (except where this is because of an error that is corrected promptly).

Examples of disciplinary cases on the grounds of a breach of Principle 5 have included the following:

- Creating a sham partnership to avoid sole practitioner requirements;
- Recklessly, but not dishonestly, misleading the court;
- Putting your own financial interests before those of the client;
- Making improper payments out of a client account;
- Failing to protect clients from mortgage fraud; and
- Making false representations on behalf of a client.

Systems and controls that should be considered to support effective governance include.

- Supervision policy;
- A compliance culture that supports an ethical response from all colleagues;
- Ensuring that there is a reporting procedure that facilitates prompt disclosures; and
- Whistleblowing policy.

Principle 6

"You act in a way that encourages equality, diversity, and inclusion."

This Principle has its origin in a number of the regulatory objectives, and we are required to apply it in employment relationships, service provision, and in our private lives. Quite often, a breach of Principle 6 will also trigger consideration of Principle 2 and duties to uphold trust and confidence and the SRA has issued guidance resources and warning notices on our equality duties and unacceptable conduct such as will arise in connection with offensive communications, sexual and other harassment etc.[5]

Case study
In 2019, a registered foreign lawyer and partner in a law firm was rebuked by the SRA after being found in an Employment Tribunal hearing to have unfairly sacked his children's nanny (on the grounds of her pregnancy).

Systems and controls that should be considered to support effective governance include:

- Equality and diversity policy;
- Training of HR staff on employment and discrimination law;
- Social media policy;
- Reporting and notification policy; and
- Whistleblowing policy.

Principle 7

"You act in the best interests of each client."

This phrase is often quoted but rarely analysed, which is risky because it is more than an aspirational affirmation. It means that you must act in good faith and do your best for each client. Circumstances that might compromise this would arise if you were unable to maintain your duty of confidentiality, acted in circumstances where there was a conflict of interest or where you did not have the competence to provide a proper standard of service, and failed to consider the client's need and attributes.

Systems and controls that should be considered to support effective governance include:

- Client inception process;
- Confidentiality and disclosure process;
- Conflicts of interest policy;
- Supervision policy; and
- Learning and development resources that enable ongoing competency training.

SRA Codes of Conduct

The STaRs contain two Codes of Conduct. These are both essential reading for the COLP as they are documents that explain the professional standards that must be met by individuals and the standards and business controls that must be implemented in authorised law firms.

The SRA Code of Conduct for Solicitors, Registered European Lawyers and Registered Foreign Lawyers

Solicitors, RELs, and RFLs all require to be registered and licensed to be able to provide legal services. Solicitors are on the roll of solicitors maintained by the SRA and need a practising certificate in force that must be renewed annually. RELs and RFLs must have their names on registers maintained by the SRA and must renew registration on an annual basis. These three categories of lawyers have a direct regulatory relationship with the SRA.

This Code of Conduct describes the standards of professionalism expected of them. They apply to the named individuals regardless of where they work. Whilst the majority of solicitors etc. are employed in authorised law firms, a significant number are employed in-house and some work overseas. All are subject to the same Code and they are personally accountable for compliance.

The SRA Code of Conduct for Firms

This Code applies to authorised law firms and speaks to the managers (and where relevant, non-manager owners), the compliance officers, and all employees of the business. The application to employees includes solicitors and extends to all other employees who may be providing legal services or be in administrative or business support roles.

There are standards in both Codes that dictate the professionalism that must be displayed. These are usually in identical form so that in many ways the separation into two Codes seems artificial and unnecessary. The reason for the separation is because solicitors, RELs, and RFLs must apply the requirements in a variety of work settings and not just when employed in private practice from SRA-authorised law firms.

Compliance officers should consider what the SRA expects and ensure that the firm's response supports all employees. In many ways this is easier to achieve than might be the case with the Principles. Policies and procedures are more obvious to identify and align with Code requirements. It is also important to note that whilst the Principles pervade a manager's or employee's personal life in some circumstances, the Codes apply to the provision of legal services only.

The following text shows the range of professional standards (with the reference points in each Code), with a commentary on risk and suggested compliance solutions to support internal conversations about risk management.

1. Code provision – Maintaining trust and acting fairly

Paragraphs 1.1, 1.2, and 1.4 of the Solicitors' Code, repeated in identical form in the Firm Code, state:

> *"You do not unfairly discriminate by allowing your personal views to affect your professional relationships and the way in which you provide your services.*
> *"You do not abuse your position by taking unfair advantage of clients*[6] *or others. You do not mislead or attempt to mislead your clients, the court or others, either by your own acts or omissions or allowing or being complicit in the acts or omissions of others (including your client)."*

Risk management

These duties apply to every authorised law firm and all managers and employees.

These duties are designed to support the SRA's brand management function; it is important that there is trust in the profession for a variety of reasons, including client confidence and the wider public interest position tied up with the profession's role as trusted advisers.

The discrimination point is significant and must not be misunderstood by compliance officers. By the wording of this requirement, the SRA is making it very clear that our duties extend beyond mere compliance with equalities legislation. The law is the starting point and regulatory requirements create higher bolt-on expectations about our behaviours. Nothing must impair impartiality and the duty to deliver legal services in a neutral way that protects and promotes the client's interests. This is an essential point to make to all colleagues and a consideration that should be borne in mind by supervisors and complaints handlers.

Nothing about client interests or instructions, or commercial considerations, should place anyone in the position where they are misusing their professional status (which extends to the status of all colleagues, regardless of role or qualification). Again, this is an essential point to convey to colleagues. If an action is deemed to be unprofessional, then it is likely that the SRA will consider it misconduct, notwithstanding any explanation as to why it might have been considered appropriate. Bearing this in mind, it is important that colleagues understand that it is sometimes acceptable to refuse to act on clients', or others', instructions. A good COLP will offer support to colleagues who may need to challenge inappropriate behaviour of this type.

Suggestions for systems and controls to support effective governance

It is not mandatory to have an equality and diversity policy, although this compliance tool is suggested in the SRA Guidance. Hints as to content are given:

- The policy should reflect the size and composition of the firm.
- It should include a commitment to the legislative and regulatory duties.
- It should acknowledge that regulatory duties impose higher standards on the firm.
- A requirement that everyone complies and a statement about the consequences of non-compliance.
- Recruitment and interviewing processes.
- Complaints handling.
- Whistleblowing.

In addition, the firm should consider having statements about equality duties in client-facing literature and a mechanism for handling client discrimination allegations. Training of HR staff on employment and discrimination law should be provided and training of all managers and employees on the law and regulation and the firm's systems and controls is also recommended. A whistleblowing policy should be drawn up.

2. Code provision – Maintaining trust and acting fairly: undertakings

Paragraph 1.3 in both Codes includes the following statement:

> *"You perform all undertakings given by you and do so within an agreed timescale or if no timescale has been agreed then within a reasonable amount of time."*

An undertaking means a statement, given orally or in writing, whether or not it includes the word "undertake" or "undertaking", to someone who reasonably places reliance on it, that you or a third party will do something or cause something to be done, or refrain from doing something.

Risk management

These duties apply to every authorised law firm and all managers and employees.

The regulatory consequences of a breached undertaking must not be underestimated. Bearing in mind that the giving of an undertaking, and the assurances that this implies, goes to the heart of concepts such as trust and confidence and integrity, the SRA takes a hard line in dealing with misconduct issues in this area.

Solicitors ought to be familiar with the concept of an undertaking, but may well need to be reminded of the exact specification and the nuances of the definition.

Non-solicitors, particularly those who are not otherwise qualified lawyers, may not appreciate when their words constitute an undertaking and the consequences for both them and the firm. The COLP will want to ensure that there are no misunderstandings and that both the giving and receiving of undertakings is tightly controlled by the firm.

Law firms need to consider the enforceability of undertakings. The case of *Harcus Sinclair LLP v. Your Lawyers Limited* (2021) UKSC 32 reminded us (albeit in *obiter dictum* narrative) that the courts do not have jurisdiction over limited company and limited liability partnership law firms and as a consequence have no power to enforce undertakings given by these entities (in contrast to the court's powers to enforce undertakings given by individual solicitors and unincorporated law firms). It would be regarded as best practice for the firm to have an agreed position on the giving and receiving of undertakings in any circumstance where this exclusion is relevant.

Case study
In 2021, a law firm and one of its partners were each fined £12,000 for failing to perform 32 undertakings given to lenders in connection with conveyancing transactions within the agreed timescales. The SDT stated that this failure had not only caused harm to the lender but also to the reputation of the profession.

Suggestions for systems and controls to support effective governance
A written undertakings policy is advisable (and in connection with some accreditation schemes is compulsory). Suggested content includes:

- A reminder about what an undertaking is;
- Clarity on who can give an undertaking and (for non-standard undertakings) wording requirements;
- Additional risk management information, including financial limits and cut-off dates;
- The firm's position about the giving of undertakings if it is a limited company or limited liability partnership/terms for receipt of the same from these bodies;
- Record-keeping requirements – consider the merits of having a central register and COLP's records as well as insisting on having file evidence; and
- Firm's requirements on the receipt of undertakings.

Training to relevant staff on this topic is suggested, perhaps to include the risks associated with ambiguous undertakings, undertakings given on behalf of clients etc., and the firm's systems and controls.

Supervisory oversight and, if necessary, reporting to the COLP, managers, and learning and development colleagues about training needs, lack of adherence to systems and controls etc. is also advisable.

3. Code provision – Dispute resolution and proceedings before courts, tribunals and inquiries

Chapter two of the Solicitors' Code sets out these duties in full. These are included in the Firm Code through reference to applicable standards described in paragraph 7.1 (a).

The requirements relate to the following issues:

- Evidence.
- Witnesses.
- Statements etc. that are put to the court.
- Not being in contempt of the court.
- Duties as officers of the court – e.g., complying with court orders, not wasting court time, drawing the court's attention to relevant and material cases etc.

Risk management

The firm must consider whether these duties apply to them (because of the types of legal services provided) and how to ensure compliance as necessary.

Where they do apply, it is essential that the COLP has the confidence that all colleagues for whom these duties are relevant understand the requirements and do nothing that may compromise compliance. This would not only be considered a possible breach of the Code-specific requirements but would also be a question of non-compliance with Principle 1, as well as Principles relating to trust, independence, honesty and integrity, and as such would be potentially a serious misconduct matter.

As with undertakings, it is hoped that solicitors and other qualified lawyers providing dispute resolution services would be familiar with their duties to the court. However, it would be unwise to assume anything and the COLP will want to take steps to satisfy themselves that colleagues will recognise inappropriate or unethical behaviour and respond correctly.

These are undoubtedly difficult judgement calls. Less experienced colleagues, or those lacking appropriate communication skills, may find professional decision-making difficult in these areas. They can be supported through mentoring and considerate supervisory support, and through training on both the professional knowledge and soft skills.

It is essential that a client's inappropriate instructions or unrealistic expectations are challenged. Duties to the court will always take precedence over duties to act in the client's best interests if these two concerns are not aligned. It is not improper, and makes for best practice, to make this clear to clients.

Suggestions for systems and controls to support effective governance

Where relevant, client care information should be adjusted to make clear that where there is an issue of professional duties to the court, and professional duties to clients, that the former will take precedence. Instructions that would be illegal or unethical might necessitate the need to terminate a retainer. These decisions should be recorded so that they can be justified.

Training should be considered for relevant fee earners on the specific content of this chapter that applies to them. Information about the support that these colleagues can expect from supervisors, the COLP, and managers should be communicated, plus the COLP's expectations regarding supervisory oversight should be made clear.

4. Code provision – Service and competence: acting on instructions

Paragraph 3.1 of the Solicitors' Code and paragraph 4.1 of the Firm Code contain identical requirements that impose personal duties that must be displayed by solicitors and all other employees, as follows:

> *"You only act for clients on instructions from the client, or from someone properly authorised to provide instructions on their behalf. If you have reason to suspect that the instructions do not represent your client's wishes, you do not act unless you have satisfied yourself that they do. However, in circumstances where you have legal authority to act, notwithstanding that it is not possible to obtain or ascertain the instructions of your client, then you are subject to the overriding obligation to protect your client's best interests."*

Risk management

One of the motivations for having a regulated legal industry is consumer protection. The incentive is that clients have confidence that we will protect and promote their interests and use our legal skills to act in their best interests.

However, in order to comply with our regulatory and professional duties, we must progress a client's matter on properly given instructions. We are, after all, agents acting on behalf of others. This fiduciary duty means that we must be able to demonstrate that our client's instructions are lawful and proper. Improper instructions might arise because a client lacks capacity or is otherwise vulnerable because they are being pressured in some way.

Acting on instructions provided by a third party increases the risks that we may as a consequence act illegally or unprofessionally. In such circumstances, it is important to be clear about correctly identifying the client and exclusively focusing on the duty to act in their best interests. We must take appropriate steps to confirm that the third party has authority to provide instructions and, where relevant, that the underlying client has provided their freely-given consent to the arrangement. Where authority is derived from a role – such as being an attorney – then evidence of the attorneyship should be obtained.

Suggestions for systems and controls to support effective governance

It is advisable that internal systems should include the means to collect evidence regarding how instructions are obtained with the need to demonstrate that where it is from a third party that the fee earner has confirmation (preferably written) that the client authorises the arrangement or, in other circumstances, that evidence of authority has been obtained and analysed.

It is best practice for the COLP to understand the SRA's position on the needs of vulnerable clients and to assess where vulnerability may manifest in terms of the services provided. Do staff in these teams need training and do systems need to show that clients' needs have been reflected in the firm's relationship with them?

Evaluate whether competency considerations trigger the need to support colleagues with training and supervisory oversight so that they are able to deal with vulnerability issues and difficult-but-necessary conversations about the ability to give instructions and/or proper authority to provide instructions on behalf of another person.

5. Code provision – Service and competence: ensuring a competent standard of service

Paragraphs in chapter three of the Solicitors' Code, repeated in part in chapter four of the Firm Code, describe services standards and competency requirements.

In the Solicitors' Code, we are told:

- *"You ensure that the service you provide to clients is competent and delivered in a timely manner.*
- *You maintain your competence to carry out your role and keep your professional knowledge and skills up to date.*
- *You consider and take account of your client's attributes, needs and circumstances."*

The wording in the Firm Code is slightly different, showing that there are the following personal duties addressed to all managers and employees in the business:

- *"You ensure that the service you provide to clients is competent and delivered in a timely manner, and takes account of your client's attributes, needs and circumstances."*

Plus, managers within the firm are directed as follows:

- *"You ensure that your managers and employees are competent to carry out their role, and keep their professional knowledge and skills, as well as understanding of their legal, ethical, and regulatory obligations, up to date."*

Risk management

Competency is tested through the application of the STaRs. In other resources, we are told that the SRA uses a broad definition of competence so that it is assessed as being the ability to perform roles and tasks to the expected standard. This requires an evaluation of an individual's role and responsibilities, and a response to the fact that competency is accrued and is a lifelong (or career-long) experience.

In terms of services to clients, the professional duty is to ensure that the individual service-provider has the necessary skill sets to protect the client's interests and to act in the client's best interests. This will not just be professional knowledge and skills but also, as can be seen from the Firm Code and the instruction to employers, extends to legal, ethical, and regulatory obligations. COLPs are well-advised to consider learning and development programmes that ensure all members of staff have access to such knowledge. Not only does this support the delivery of good-quality legal services, with the commercial and reputational benefits that this brings, but a commitment to firmwide education supports the COLP and managers, and demonstrates to the SRA that their intentions are to foster an appropriate compliance culture.

These duties also address service standards. This is important to the COLP. Complaints of poor service are of course considered by the Legal Ombudsman, but this body does discuss issues of potential misconduct with the SRA.

Questions for the COLP to address include:

- Do our staff have sufficient time to provide a proper standard of service, or are we asking too much of them?
- Do our staff have adequate resources to deliver a proper standard of service or do they lack business support that will undermine their client relationships?
- Do we deliver a service that does not take into account individual clients' needs?
- Do we support our staff to consider individual clients and their needs so that changes in service style and delivery are accommodated?

- Specifically, have we considered whether we provide services to vulnerable clients and can we show that we protect their interests in an appropriate way?

Case study
In 2021, a solicitor described as "deplorable" was struck off the roll of solicitors, and ordered to pay costs of £20,000 because of the harm his misconduct had caused personal injury clients whose claims were struck out. The SDT said, "The Tribunal found the extent and repeated nature of the respondent's failures deplorable. They could only be described as manifest incompetence."

Suggestions for systems and controls to support effective governance
These duties can be managed through the following:

- Training programmes to ensure appropriate technical and regulatory knowledge is accessible.
- A business strategy that ensures that the firm is well-run so that resources are adequate.
- A compliance culture that enables managers and employees to seek support.
- Supervisory oversight and feedback mechanisms.

6. Code provision – Service and competence: supervision
Paragraphs 3.5 and 3.6 of the Solicitors' Code speak directly to solicitors, RELs, and RFLs delivering a significant regulatory message:

> *"Where you supervise or manage others providing legal services:*
> *(a) you remain accountable for the work carried out through them; and*
> *(b) you effectively supervise work being done for clients.*
> *You ensure that the individuals you manage are competent to carry out their role, and keep their professional knowledge and skills, as well as understanding of their legal, ethical and regulatory obligations, up to date."*

This personal duty is twinned with responsibilities imposed on managers in paragraph 4.4 of the Firm Code:

> *"You have an effective system for supervising clients' matters."*

Risk management

It is important to note that the SRA imposes accountability duties on solicitors (and others) who perform supervisory functions, without providing any defining language with which to determine what being a supervisor is or what is included in their supervisory, or managerial, roles. Language like "remain accountable", "effectively supervise", and "ensure" must be given due consideration as they expose the supervisor to the need to justify their response to the roles. Similarly, the overarching obligation on the authorised firm is equally vague but instructional; your systems for supervision must be effective.

This requires the COLP to ensure that policies and procedures are implemented that are effective in countering the risk that there is a lack of appropriate oversight and support of individuals. What is effective will therefore be a combination of considering individual needs plus the needs of clients and how the firm delivers legal services.

Whilst this is partly a judgement call based on the firm's peculiar circumstances, there are some universal truths that should be acknowledged:

- Done properly, supervision of others involves the allocation of time and resources to the supervisor. This is not to be regarded as a bolt-on responsibility that should be done only if time allows.
- Effective supervision requires more than just knowledge of the law. It also requires knowledge of legal, regulatory, and professional duties. The supervisor must also be an effective communicator; being a supervisor means that the role-holder acts as an ambassador for the managers of the firm, ensuring that the colleagues they supervise understand the firm's expectations but also ensuring that managers are provided with information necessary to support the firm's authorised status.
- Supervision should be evidenced with attendance notes and other records.
- The individual who is supervised should understand the contribution that they make to an effective process. Again, communication skills are needed.
- No one is too senior or too experienced not to be supervised. Rather, the supervision process should be adaptable to meet individual needs and circumstances.
- Done well, supervision supports the COLP and managers with their responsibilities.

- Done well, supervision supports the one-voice feel of the firm, which has both commercial and reputational benefits.

Case study

In 2022, a solicitor was rebuked for failing to supervise an immigration caseworker colleague in a matter that led the High Court to refer the law firm to the SRA. The supervisor admitted that it was his misconduct that led to a judicial review application being made that was not properly arguable and that undermined the operation of the immigration system. The case-handler and the supervisor were based in different offices of the firm, many miles apart. The SRA determined that a disciplinary finding was necessary "to uphold the public's confidence and deter similar behaviour in the future".

The same solicitor had previously been banned from holding compliance roles after the SRA found that he had ignored anti-money laundering responsibilities. On that occasion he had been fined £25,000 (later reduced because of his limited means) and the law firm had been fined £15,000.

Suggestions for systems and controls to support effective governance

Unquestionably, the SRA expects supervision to be a visible and effective risk management tool and holds individuals and the firm personally and collectively responsible for this.

There should be a supervision policy to ensure oversight of the quality of service provision, and also to oversee compliance with legal and regulatory duties, and to ensure the development of competencies on the part of the individuals being supervised. The objectives should be clearly stated and should be measurable.

However, simply having a well-worded policy will not be sufficient. The COLP should consider whether training is needed so that managers and employees understand their various roles in the supervision process. Do resources need to be reallocated to enable supervision? Do individuals need to be trained in skills that support them in responding suitably to supervision?

7. Code provision – Client money and assets

For solicitors, RELs, and RFLs working in SRA-authorised firms, and for all managers and employees in the firm, both Codes contain identical duties (in chapter four of the Solicitors' Code and in chapter five of the Firm Code):

- *"You properly account to clients for any financial benefit you receive as a result of their instructions, except where they have agreed otherwise.*
- *You safeguard money and assets entrusted to you by clients and others."*

A financial benefit is defined as meaning any commission, discount or rebate. The meaning of assets is also defined (but often overlooked in firm's risk management procedures). We are told by the SRA that it includes money, documents, wills, deeds, investments, and other property.

Risk management
The firm-wide, and employee-wide, duty to safeguard money and assets has significance for both the COLP and the COFA. For the COLP, it requires a consideration of financial stability and business viability; does anything about the business place the protection of client money and assets in jeopardy? Is the firm screening staff sufficiently thoroughly to ensure that an employee does not pose a threat? Is training adequate to ensure that relevant staff understand the issues regarding the holding of client money, and the storage of client property?

Suggestions for systems and controls to support effective governance
No one in the firm should be allowed to misunderstand the significance of messages about client money that are addressed to them personally. This is an important message to be disseminated to everyone.

The mechanics of risk management are largely included in the SRA Accounts Rules and consequently within the COFA's responsibilities. However, the COLP will want to be satisfied on strategy, and the impact that this has on financial stability and business viability matters, and have confidence that nothing about the management of the firm will jeopardise compliance with these duties to manage risks associated with holding client money.

8. Code provision – Referrals and introductions
Both Codes of Conduct contain duties that apply when a client is referred to a solicitor or the firm, or the solicitor/firm makes an introduction of a client to a third party. The duties are described in detail in paragraphs 5.1 and 5.2 of the Solicitors' Code, and by reference in the Firm Code, which states that the firm must have the same standards described in paragraph 7.1(b). We are told that in respect of referrals of clients to a third party, and in respect of any introductions to you or with whom you share your fees:

- You must ensure that clients are informed of any financial or other interest that concerns the referral;
- Clients must be informed of any relevant fee sharing arrangement;
- A fee sharing agreement must be in writing;
- No payments must be given or received in respect of clients requiring criminal law services;
- There must be no breach of publicity restrictions contained in the SRA Codes; and
- Where a referral fee is made or received, it will be treated as a fee within the meaning of section 57(7) of the Legal Aid, Sentencing and Punishment of Offenders Act.

A referral is not defined by the SRA, but the term "introducer" is and the SRA says that this "*means any person, business, or organisation who or that introduces or refers clients to your business, or recommends your business to clients or otherwise puts you and clients in touch with each other*".

A referral fee is defined by reference to legislation.

Risk management

Improper referral arrangements are likely to concern the SRA as it will consider whether the scheme has harmed trust and confidence in the profession (and, as a consequence, breached Principle 2) because clients trust us to protect their interests and this extends to recommendations we may make or act upon. The SRA will also consider the impact on Principle 3, and the duty of independence that we must never allow to be compromised by our commercial arrangements with third parties, and of course Principle 7 and the duty to always act in an individual client's best interests.

Referral arrangements therefore need careful monitoring by the COLP; the duties in the Codes are designed to ensure that nothing about these arrangements compromises duties to clients. Clients must also be given appropriate information about the arrangement so that they are able to make an informed choice about the referral.

The Codes are silent on the point of referral fees that are prohibited by law. This is because your compliance with the law is required as part of the regulatory arrangements. Elsewhere, the SRA states:

> "*In addition to the regulatory requirements set by us in our Codes, Principles and our rules and regulations, we directly monitor and enforce the*

requirements relating to referral fees set out in section 56 of the Legal Aid, Sentencing and Punishment of Offenders Act 2012."

The SRA has produced guidance to explain how the law is applied and their regulatory powers in this regard.[7]

The COLP will want to know about all referral arrangements in existence and have the confidence that these are being monitored and that clients are receiving correct information. The COLP will also need to take a view on the legal override and be satisfied that illegal referral fees are not being paid or received.

Case study

In 2022, a solicitor was rebuked for accepting referrals from a third party that acquired clients in a way that would have been a breach of SRA requirements if undertaken by a solicitor or law firm. Solicitors and law firms are not allowed to make unsolicited approaches to potential clients. The solicitor rebuked was aware that the third party used unsolicited and targeted approaches to individuals who were then introduced to the law firm. The SRA decided that a rebuke was a necessary sanction in order "to uphold public confidence in the delivery of legal services".

Suggestions for systems and controls to support effective governance

A documented Introductions and Referrals Policy would be appropriate, with perhaps pre-drafted letters to ensure clients are informed of relevant information.

9. Code provision – Separate businesses

Both Codes of Conduct contain duties that apply when a client is referred to a separate business, or the client's matter is divided between the authorised firm and a separate business. The duties are described in detail in paragraph 5.3 of the Solicitors' Code, and by reference in the Firm Code, which states that the firm must have the same standards (confirmed in paragraph 7.1(b)).

The duty is as follows:

"You only:

a) Refer, recommend or introduce a client to a separate business; or

b) Divide, or allow to be divided, a client's matter between you and a separate business;

Where the client has given informed consent to your doing so."

Clearly, it is necessary to understand what a "separate business" is, and the SRA provides the following definition, which applies to the managers and employees of authorised firms in circumstance where there is a separate business:

a) *"Which you own;*
b) *Which you are owned by;*
c) *Where you actively participate in the provision of its services, including where you have any direct control over the business or any indirect control over the business through another person, or*
d) *Which you are connected with,*
e) *And which is not an authorised body, an authorised non-SRA firm, or an overseas practice."*

Risk management

These provisions reflect the fact that managers and employees (solicitors and non-solicitors) are able to have interests in businesses that are not authorised by the SRA. However, it is necessary to protect clients of the law firm, and customers of the separate business, so that they understand the type of protections they will obtain when receiving services from each businesses. The fact that there might be a connection with a solicitor and with a regulated business must not be allowed to create misunderstandings.

Suggestions for systems and controls to support effective governance

The COLP must be confident that they have identified any separate businesses.

Thereafter, suggestions for monitoring compliance include:

- An audit and register of all separate businesses connected with the firm.
- Checks of incoming managers and employees to keep the register current.
- Systems and checklists to ensure that, if relevant, clients/customers are provided with appropriate information.
- Incorporating checks into file review response.
- Training of relevant staff about the regulatory duties and the firm's internal response.

10. Code provision – conflict of interests

Both Codes of Conduct describe professional duties in respect of conflict of interests with identical wording, thereby imposing identical duties on solicitors, RELs, RFLs, and all other managers and employees within the business. These duties are described in paragraphs 6.1 and 6.2 of each Code.

We are asked to consider two scenarios. Firstly, we are required to identify own interest conflict of interests, both actual and where there is a significant risk of such a conflict, and not act. Secondly, we are required to identify client interest conflicts, or significant risk of client conflicts, and not act unless we can make use of one of two exceptions known as the substantially common interest and the competing for the same objective exception. If an exception is used to continue to act, notwithstanding the existence of a conflict or a significant risk of a conflict, then this is subject to meeting prescriptive conditions.

A number of defined phrases support understanding of these duties:

- An own interest conflict means any situation where your duty to act in the best interest of any client in relation to a matter conflicts, or there is a significant risk that it may conflict, with your own interests in relation to that or a related matter.
- Conflict of interest means a situation where your separate duties to act in the best interests of two or more clients in relation to the same or a related matters conflict (i.e., a client conflict of interests).
- Substantially common interest means a situation where there is a clear common purpose and a strong consensus on how it is to be achieved.
- Competing for the same objective is described as any situation in which two or more clients are competing for an "objective" which, if attained by one client, will make that "objective" unattainable to the other client or clients, and "objective" means an asset, contract or business opportunity which two or more clients are seeking to acquire or recover through a liquidation (or some other form of insolvency process) or by means of an auction or tender process or a bid or offer, but not a public takeover.

Risk management

Analysing conflicts of interest correctly is one of the most essential ethical decisions that the COLP and the law firm need to manage. Acting correctly supports you to demonstrate not only compliance with the Codes but also with many of the Principles, including trust and confidence, integrity, and of course the duty to act in the best interests of each client.

The definitions provided by the SRA help to a degree, but it is also important that the nuances of the wording are also part of the conflict decision process. For example, we need to consider not only actual but also significant risks of conflicts arising. We also need to consider conflicts in the context of both the same matter and also related matters.

The COLP will want to have confidence that:

- Conflicts searches are both undertaken and analysed.
- That individuals consider all possible own interest conflicts.
- That the absolute prohibition on acting in an own interest scenario is not flouted.
- That the client conflict regime is understood, and that the exceptions are used with care.
- That colleagues understand what a high-risk scenario is and involve the COLP in definitions which are made when these are identified.

Case study

In 2022, a solicitor acted in the purchase of a residential property for Client A who was the solicitor's step-sister, and also for Client B who was his father and was providing the completion monies by way of a loan agreement with a company of which he was a director. This company was described as a regular client of the solicitor's law firm. Upon investigation, the solicitor admitted that he acted in a conflict of interest. The SRA rebuked him, noting also that the individual had failed to follow his firm's client onboarding process, had not provided Client A with client care documentation, had not advised the two clients, and had failed to check sources of funds.

Suggestions for systems and controls to support effective governance

In the SRA Handbook (2011-2019), the SRA included a requirement for mandatory systems and controls to manage conflict of interests, which included training of staff. This is not replicated in the STaRs, but the COLP should consider the merits of this response.

A written conflicts policy might include the following content:

- A reminder about the SRA definitions and our duties.
- The firm's policy about conflicts risk management.
- Registration of particular own interests.
- Statement of the firm's policy in acting in high-risk scenarios, e.g., acting for buyer and seller in conveyancing transactions etc.
- Statement of the firm's policy on acting for two or more clients in conflict-of-interest situations in circumstances where the exceptions exist.
- The role of the COLP in decision-making.
- The firm's requirements in respect of conflict searches etc., and the expectation for ongoing monitoring of initial compliance analysis.

Consider also the introduction of a register of interests to require the recording of own interest conflicts, plus the training of all staff on the regulatory duties plus the conflict search practices, and supervisory oversight of conflict decision-making.

11. Code provision – Confidentiality

As with conflict of interests, the SRA's requirements about confidentiality are in identical form at paragraph 6.3 of each of the Codes of Conduct:

> *"You keep the affairs of current and former clients confidential unless disclosure is required or permitted by law or the client consents."*

Risk management

This duty is simply expressed but profoundly significant to the COLP. The extent of this duty must not be misunderstood by anyone in the firm; whoever they are, whatever their specific role, this duty of confidentiality vests in them both as a current and then eventually a former colleague.

COLPs need to reflect on how breaches of confidentiality can occur – human error, idle gossip, overheard conversations, lost files, cyber breaches, working away from the office, outsourcing arrangements with insufficient confidentiality terms – and must ensure that risk management procedures are rolled out as mitigation.

All risk management needs to acknowledge that this is an aspect of professionalism where mistakes will happen (emails will be sent to the wrong recipient or with the wrong attachments, papers do get mislaid and lost etc.). Where the COLP, and the managers of the firm, acknowledge that this is the case, and encourage openness and accountability, then there is more confidence that issues will be reported.

The COLP will also want to manage the second part of this professional duty and have confidence that disclosure of confidential information is suitably controlled. This may involve discussions with the firm's money laundering reporting officer in respect of AML disclosures.

Case study

In 2021, a solicitor was fined for various misconduct issues including the fly-tipping of legal documents that contained confidential information. The SRA said:

> *"The public would not expect a solicitor to put clieant information at risk in this way, and such a failure in data management is likely to impact public trust in the provision of legal services. The public expect their private information to be treated in the utmost confidence by the profession."*

Suggestions for systems and controls to support effective governance

A written confidentiality policy is recommended as best practice and can include the following content:

- A reminder about the regulatory duties on confidentiality.
- The firm's policy about confidentiality risk management.
- A procedure (ideally involving the COLP) for management of decisions about disclosure of confidential information (with signposting to the firm's money laundering reporting officer and AML policies as appropriate).
- How to report breaches of duty.
- Social media risk management.

Associated systems and controls can be used to align with data protection risk management, retention, and storage and safe destruction of client information and records, disclosure duties, and use of information barriers.

A separate social media policy is also recommended to cover the following points:

- Duties of confidentiality.
- Inappropriate communications.

- Offensive communications.
- Regulatory reach to personal social media usage.
- Any consequences of breach in terms of reputational issues and employment contract.

Training of all staff is advisable, so that the breadth of the confidentiality duty is understood and there is awareness of the firm's expectations and risk management controls.

Risk management can also be supported by internal reporting procedures so that breaches are reported promptly and with supervisory oversight.

12. Code provision – Disclosure duties

This is another professional duty that applies to everyone in the firm (although in practice, it is usually going to arise in respect of the lawyer–client relationship) and so is described in identical terms in paragraph 6.4 of both Codes, as follows:

> *"Where you are acting for a client on a matter, you make the client aware of all information material to the matter of which you have knowledge, except when:*
>
> *a) The disclosure of the information is prohibited by legal restrictions imposed in the interests of national security or the prevention of crime;*
>
> *b) Your client gives informed consent, given or evidenced in writing, to the information not being disclosed to them;*
>
> *c) You have reason to believe that serious physical or mental injury will be caused to your client or another if the information is disclosed; or*
>
> *d) The information is contained in a privileged document that you have knowledge of only because it has been mistakenly disclosed."*

Risk management

This duty is described in its default setting; it is the duty to make full disclosure of material information to current clients of the firm so that they are in a position to make informed decisions regarding their instructions.

The SRA chooses not to explain what is meant by "material" but it is safe to assume that this applies to information that supports the client in their decision-making so it is relevant to the specific retainer and not simply of inconsequential interest.

This duty can be varied in the circumstances described in the Codes. The most relevant variation is described at paragraph 6.4 (b) and this is where the client to whom disclosure is owed gives informed consent to non-disclosure. However, the COLP will want to oversee that this measure is taken only in circumstances where it is reasonable to ask to vary the retainer, and ensure that this agreement is written, and that consequently the scope of the retainer is revised.

The COLP will also want to be satisfied that if this default position has been varied because the material information is confidential to another current or former client, that the firm is able to protect the confidential information from accidental disclosure. The SRA's expectation is that the firm will take appropriate measures and is silent on this specific point, except where the circumstances are such that clients have adverse interests.

Suggestions for systems and controls to support effective governance

This is relevant to fee earners who need to understand the regulatory duties imposed on them and what steps must be taken if they identify that a conflict of duties has arisen (i.e., their duty of confidentiality is not reconcilable with their duty of disclosure), the need to factor this consideration when accepting instructions, and the need to be vigilant for an issue arising during the course of the retainer.

The firm should have a policy on the use of information barriers (and it is acknowledged that it is a suitable risk management technique to refuse any instructions where a conflict of duties is identified).

Supervisory oversight will also support compliance and risk management.

13. Code provision – Conflict of confidentiality and disclosure duties

Again, this is in identical format in both Codes, so that at paragraph 6.5 we are told:

> *"You do not act for a client in a matter where that client has an interest adverse to the interest of another current or former client of you or your business or employer, for whom you or your business or employer holds confidential information which is material to that matter, unless:*
>
> *a) Effective measures have been taken which result in there being no real risk of disclosure of the confidential information; or*
>
> *b) The current or former client whose information you or your business or employer holds has given informed consent, given or evidenced in writing, to you acting, including to any measures taken to protect their information."*

Risk management

Adversity – or, to be specific, "an interest adverse" – is not defined but the SRA has always suggested that we should apply the common law meaning to this.

Paragraph 6.5 prohibits acting in this situation unless one of the two exceptions are satisfied. Exception (a) applies if effective measures are put in place. This is a high-risk strategy; the courts take a hard approach to this as has been evidenced from recent cases. Exception (b) could be seen as being less risky as it involves the current/former client to whom confidentiality being involved.

All COLPs should want to have involvement in any decisions where the firm decides to act, notwithstanding the existence of adversity.

Suggestions for systems and controls to support effective governance

The COLP will want to be satisfied that there is an agreed response to this type of conflict of duties. This could be an absolute prohibition on acting in such circumstances; it could be a decision to proceed that the COLP alone can make and the COLP decides what safeguards must be erected; it could be a decision that the COLP is happy to delegate to others (although this is the higher risk response and a prudent COLP would want to at least be informed of such decisions and be confident that colleagues understand their duties).

Template letters for seeking client consent to disclosure of confidential information or non-disclosure of material information or use of information barriers would be advisable.

14. Code provision – Cooperation and accountability: personal duties

Paragraph 7.1 of the Solicitors' Code and paragraph 3.1 of the Firm Code contains the identical requirement that "*you keep up to date with and follow the law and regulation governing the way you work*".

Additionally, paragraph 7.2 of the Solicitors' Code informs solicitors, RELs, and RFLs that you must be "*able to justify your decisions and actions in order to demonstrate compliance with your obligations under the SRA's regulatory arrangements*".

Risk management

Risk management will be demonstrated in a firm that itself keeps up to speed with the SRA's regulatory arrangements and ensures that relevant information is cascaded, in appropriate language, to colleagues.

The extra duty imposed on directly regulated individuals carefully uses the word "justify" to explain what the SRA might be seeking when demanding information about their actions. Bear in mind that to justify will mean to demonstrate that an action was reasonable, and it is clear that the COLP should consider insisting on accurate and contemporaneous record-keeping, attendance notes, and similar.

Suggestions for systems and controls to support effective governance

It seems unlikely that the firm, and individuals within the firm, will be able to demonstrate compliance with these duties without recourse to training and development resources, and without there being requirements relating to file management. Effective supervisory oversight will support the achievement of these duties.

15. Code provision – Cooperation and accountability: reporting regime

Much of the remainder of chapter seven of the Solicitors' Code states the SRA's expectations about the relationship between these regulated individuals with not only it, but also other stakeholders such as the Office for Legal Complaints and the Information Commissioner's Office, when enquiries and investigations are being discussed. The Firm Code contains the same duties in chapter three, so that these duties are imposed on everyone in the authorised business.

In summary, the duties require that all solicitors, RELs, and RFLs and other managers and employees:

- *"Cooperate with the SRA, other regulators, ombudsmen, and those bodies with a role overseeing and supervising the delivery of, or investigating concerns in relation to, legal services.*
- *Respond promptly to the SRA and:*
  - *provide full and accurate explanations, information, and documents in response to any request or requirement; and*
  - *ensure that relevant information which is held by you, or by third parties carrying out functions on your behalf, which are critical to the delivery of your legal services, is available for inspection by the SRA.*
- *Do not attempt to prevent anyone from providing information to the SRA or any other body exercising regulatory, supervisory, investigatory, or prosecutory functions in the public interest.*
- *Report promptly to the SRA or another approved regulator, as appropriate, any facts or matters that you reasonably believe are capable of amounting*

to a serious breach of their regulatory arrangements by any person regulated by them (including you).

- *Inform the SRA promptly of any facts or matters that you reasonably believe should be brought to its attention in order that it may investigate whether a serious breach of its regulatory arrangements has occurred or otherwise exercise its regulatory powers.*
- *Do not subject anyone to detrimental treatment for making or proposing to make a report or provide information.*
- *Act promptly to take any remedial action requested by the SRA. If requested to do so by the SRA you investigate whether there have been any serious breaches that should be reported to the SRA."*

The Solicitors' Code also makes the point, at paragraph 7.12, that any obligations to notify or provide information to the SRA will be satisfied if the individual provides information to the firm's compliance officers on the understanding that they will make any necessary communication. This is not repeated in identical form in the Firm Code, although the duties relating to compliance and business systems in chapter 2 of this Code do imply the need to consider notification mechanisms

Risk management

These provisions are significant; they impose reporting and cooperation duties on regulated and non-regulated individuals, plus the authorised law firm itself.

Our acceptance of this type of relationship is key to the success of risk-based regulation, yet it may be a hard sell to the regulated community made easier where there is trust in the regulator and any next steps. Bear in mind that any lack of cooperation is likely to have consequences for the COLP, and managers of the business.

It is sensible for senior members of the business to encourage confidence in the regulatory regime and the relationship with the SRA and to facilitate prompt reporting of breaches, concerns, and queries within the business. Partly, this will be achieved through the creation of a reporting mechanism but, mostly, it will be dependent on the COLP and managers developing the correct compliance culture with support built-in. This is achieved through the actions of these individuals plus development initiatives that enable all colleagues to understand what the SRA does, why the SRA is interested in them, and what the firm's response is.

The significance of the reference to detrimental treatment must be noted by the COLP. It explains the SRA's concerns regarding the misuse or overuse of non-disclosure agreements by law firms and any discriminatory or unfair behaviours within the business. The COLP will want to ensure that managers, HR colleagues, and others with a role in employment decisions are made aware of this. Any Employment Tribunal findings that managers or employees have been treated unfairly must be reported to the SRA and may well trigger disciplinary interest and action.

Case study

In 2022, a sole practitioner who tried to settle a client's complaints on condition that they did not report his firm to the SRA was rebuked for misconduct. He conceded that he had acted in breach of paragraph 7.5 of the SRA Code of Conduct for Solicitors. The SRA stated that the individual was a senior solicitor and that public sanction was necessary to uphold public trust and confidence.

Suggestions for systems and controls to support effective governance

It is in the COLP's interests to ensure that there are systems and controls that facilitate early reporting of notifiable events, so that next steps can be team steps. Similarly, the COLP will want to ensure that no one is an obstacle to an open relationship with the regulator should it request information etc.

Raising awareness through training is advisable, as is a whistleblowing policy and an equality policy dealing with bullying/detrimental treatment. The relevant staff – including the HR team – should be made aware of the risks associated with improper use of non-disclosure agreements.

16. Code provision – Cooperation and accountability: openness with clients

Paragraph 7.11 of the Solicitors' Code and paragraph 3.5 of the Firm Code contain identical duties that apply to circumstances when a mistake is made in a client's matter:

> *"You are honest and open with clients if things go wrong, and if a client suffers loss or harm as a result, you put matters right (if possible) and explain fully and promptly what has happened and the likely impact. If requested to do so by the SRA you investigate whether anyone may have a claim against you, provide the SRA with a report on the outcome of your investigation, and notify relevant persons that they may have such a claim, accordingly."*

Risk management

This is an important duty and the COLP will want to exert tight control over it. The requirement that we will be "honest and open" will not of course be disregarded by anyone displaying the correct ethical behaviours. This goes to the heart of what it means to act with "trust and confidence" (Principle 2), with independence (Principle 3), honesty (Principle 4), integrity (Principle 5), and in the client's best interests (Principle 7).

This expectation will need to be reconciled with considerations regarding next steps – does the individual or the business now have an own interest conflict or a significant risk of an own interest conflict, and what should be discussed with insurers are two obvious discussions points.

COLPs should consider the SDT case of *SRA v. Howell Jones LLP* (2018) SDT 11846 in which the Tribunal decided that the law firm should not have continued to act after a client had complained such that there now existed an own interest conflict scenario, plus SRA Guidance on the topic.[8] More than anything else, the COLP will want to ensure that matters are identified and internal reports are made promptly and next steps are in accordance with an agreed firm-wide formula.

Suggestions for systems and controls to support effective governance

The implementation of an internal reporting procedure, which is understood by all colleagues.

17. Code provision – Cooperation and accountability: reporting of certain circumstances to the SRA

Paragraph 7.6 of the Solicitors' Code states that the SRA expects to be notified promptly if a solicitor, REL or RFL is:

> *"Subject to any criminal charge, conviction or caution (subject to the Rehabilitation of Offenders Act 1974); a relevant insolvency event occurs; or if the individual becomes aware of any material changes to the information previously provided to the SRA (about them personally, their practice, or any change of information on the registers maintained by the SRA), and if the individual becomes aware that information about them or their practice is or may be false, misleading, inaccurate or inaccurate."*

The Firm Code includes a similar reporting obligation that extends not only to individuals within the business but also the business itself. These duties are contained in paragraphs 3.6. 3.7, 3.8, and 3.9 where the references to "you" are addressed to the business itself:

"You notify the SRA promptly:

(a) of any indicators of serious financial difficulty relating to you; (b) if a relevant insolvency event[9] *occurs in relation to you; (c) if you intend to, or become aware that you will, cease operating as a legal business; (d) of any change to information recorded in the register.*[10]

"You provide to the SRA an information report on an annual basis or such other period as specified by the SRA in the prescribed form and by the prescribed date.

"You notify the SRA promptly if you become aware: (a) of any material changes to information previously provided to the SRA, by you or on your behalf, about you or your managers, owners or compliance officers; and (b) that information provided to the SRA, by you or on your behalf, about you or your managers, owners or compliance officers is or may be false, misleading, incomplete or inaccurate.

"You report promptly to the SRA, or another approved regulator, as appropriate, any facts or matters that you reasonably believe are capable of amounting to a serious breach of their regulatory arrangements by any person regulated by them (including you) of which you are aware. If requested to do so by the SRA, you investigate whether there have been any serious breaches that should be reported to the SRA."

There are a number of defined terms hidden in plain sight in these duties.

- The phrase "relevant insolvency" is defined by the SRA and is heavily detailed in nature. It needs to be understood by individuals and the authorised entity, both in respect of itself and in relation to managers, compliance officers, and employees.
- The reference to registers includes the roll of solicitors, the register of European lawyers, the register of foreign lawyers, and the register of authorised bodies.
- Approved regulators are those regulatory bodies that are enabled under the Legal Services Act.

Risk management

Based on the premise that the SRA is tasked with managing the risks of individuals providing legal services and law firms being authorised to do this, it is understandable that it would need to be notified of certain matters that might lead to a reconsideration of authorisation decisions.

This is a public interest point and also connected with the management of the profession's reputation as one that is completely trustworthy. Anything less than a demonstration of prompt and accountable reporting is likely to jeopardise an individual's personal position and create interest in their employer. The authorised business must also understand what triggers the SRA's renewed interest in it.

Losing authorisation status, or authorisation being altered by imposed conditions, will have an impact of whether and/or how legal services can be provided. It is imperative that the COLP and managers have confidence that everyone understands the part that they play in managing this duty. Bear in mind that this level of interest might not be understood – more experienced practitioners might have failed to understand this type of regulation and the way in which things have changed with the passing of the regulatory baton to the SRA. Non-solicitors working in your business cannot be expected to fully appreciate the SRA's interest in them.

The COLP will also want to consider whether the firm employs lawyers who are directly regulated by other approved regulators. Full details of the approved regulator regime are available from the Legal Services Board's website,[11] but will need to consider the position of any barristers, legal executives, licensed conveyancers, patent attorneys, trademark attorneys, costs lawyers, notaries, and chartered accountants that might be managers or employees of the business. Both the COLP and these individuals need to consider whether breaches of SRA duties must be reported to other approved regulators.

Suggestions for systems and controls to support effective governance

Managers and employees need to be made aware of reportable events. HR and other staff involved in recruitment need to understand what matters should be brought to the attention of the COLP and managers. Compliance can be supported through an internal reporting procedure, the development of a compliance culture that enables openness and accountability, and a whistleblowing policy.

With regard to reportable events about the authorised law firm, a standing item on risk management and other appropriate managerial meetings should support early reporting.

18. Code provision – Providing services to the public: client identification

Paragraph 8.1 of the Solicitors' Code is repeated in identical form by reference in paragraph 7.1 (c) of the Firm Code: "*You identify who you are acting for in relation to any matter*".

Risk management

This is a duty introduced by the SRA in 2019 in the STaRs. It is similar to, but less prescriptive than, the obligation to know your client for anti-money laundering purposes.

The duty has been added to our regulatory requirements because of the need to manage risks such as those associated with being used for fraudulent purposes. The chances of being used as an instrument of fraud are considerably reduced if the firm has made efforts to satisfy itself that it knows who it is dealing with and that this is part of the onboarding process.

Because it is a relatively new requirement, the SRA has issued guidance[12] that should support the COLP in deciding what measures to introduce. The guidance note contains a precautionary message, reflecting the need to be able to justify decision-making, which should be heeded by the COLP:

> *"Whatever the firm decides, it is important to ensure that all their fee-earners know what is expected of them. Depending on the circumstances, it may also be advisable to make a note on the file as to your reasons (e.g., if you depart from the process in your firm, or it is left to your discretion), bearing in mind that the onus will be on you to explain your approach should your conduct be called in to question."*

Suggestions for systems and controls to support effective governance

Most firms are subject to the Money Laundering Regulations and are familiar with client identification and verification duties necessary to comply with statutory duties. Many such firms ensure that this client due diligence is applied throughout the firm. In these circumstances, this will be sufficient to meet regulatory identification requirements as well.

A procedure should be included in the client onboarding and file opening process to ensure that these checks are made. Supervisory oversight will support these initiatives.

19. Code provision – Providing services to the public: complaints handling

Paragraphs 8.2-8.5 of the Solicitors' Code, applied in identical form by reference in paragraph 7.1 (c) of the Firm Code, state regulatory and professional duties to operate a complaints handling procedure and to signpost clients to the Legal Ombudsman if necessary.

In summary, the requirements are as follows:

- The firm has a complaint handling procedure in which managers and employees participate.
- Clients are given written information at the time of engagement about their right to complain, how to complain, and about the Legal Ombudsman's role.
- In the first instance you will be expected to consider the client's complaint. If the complaint has not been resolved to the client's satisfaction within eight weeks, they must be informed (i.e. signposted) about the right to complain to the Legal Ombudsman, with relevant practical information about time limits etc., the fact that you cannot settle the complaint, and details of alternative dispute resolution services, and whether the firm would be prepared to use such a service.
- Complaints must be handled promptly, fairly, and without charge to the complainant.

Risk management

In many ways, this is a clunky read for the COLP, both because of the prescriptive language which explains (in a way that is not consistent with the style of the majority of the Code) how the duty will be achieved, and also because of the extent of the information that must be provided (e.g., the reference to alternative dispute bodies regardless of whether the firm chooses to use such a body). This clunkiness can be attributed to requirements in the Legal Services Act.

The importance of fair complaint handling to the SRA is significant. Included in its own regulatory objectives is the need to consider consumer protection and the public interest. Mishandling of complaints is likely to place solicitors and law firms in breach of fundamental ethical behaviours as described in the SRA principles, particularly those that apply to trust and confidence, honesty, integrity, and acting in the client's best interests.

How a client is treated in respect of the handling of the matter, and thereafter, requires more specific Code-induced behaviours such as those relating to maintaining trust and acting fairly and issues concerned with client needs and attributes (particularly where the client might be considered vulnerable).

Unfortunately, or perhaps deliberately, the SRA has chosen not to define the meaning of "complaint" but it would be the foolhardy for the COLP and the firm not to have an agreed meaning with which to work. In the SRA Handbook (2011-2019) it was defined and there seems no reason why this definition should not be used still so that a complaint "*means an oral or written expression of dissatisfaction which alleges that the complainant has suffered (or may suffer) financial loss, distress, inconvenience or other detriment*".

Suggestions for systems and controls to support effective governance

The COLP will want to ensure that all complaints are handled promptly and consistently. A written complaints procedure is advisable, and this should be in a form that can be made available to clients. The procedure should be drafted in language that the client will find easy to understand. It should be responsive to the needs of individual clients, particularly those who may be vulnerable, so that, for example, complaints can be made by any reasonable method.

Training on the complaints procedure should be given to staff, and it may be preferred to have a designated complaints handler (maybe the COLP or perhaps a manager) to ensure consistency and to monitor for patterns of poor behaviour or training needs.

20. Code provision – Providing services to the public: client information

Paragraphs 8.6, 8.7, 8.10, and 8.11 of the Solicitors' Code, applied in identical form by reference in paragraph 7.1 (c) of the Firm Code, are the client care duties set by the SRA. These are as follows:

- *"You give clients information in a way they can understand. You ensure they are in a position to make informed decisions about the services they need, how their matter will be handled and the options available to them.*
- *You ensure that clients receive the best possible information about how their matter will be priced and, both at the time of engagement and when appropriate as their matter progresses, about the likely overall cost of the matter and any costs incurred.*
- *You ensure that clients understand whether and how the services you provide are regulated. This includes:*
    - *Explaining which activities will be carried out by you, as an authorised person;*
    - *Explaining which services provided by you, your business or employer, and any separate business are regulated by an approved regulator; and*
    - *Ensuring that you do not represent any business or employer which is not authorised by the SRA, including any separate business, as being regulated by the SRA.*
    - *You ensure that clients understand the regulatory protections available to them."*

Risk management

Providing information about service delivery in a way that enables the client to make informed decisions about their situation and next steps, without any surprises along the way, is a basic duty. Unfortunately, it is all too easy for a firm to respond in an unsatisfactory way. Overuse of template client care literature, information presented in a way that suits the firm rather than the client, not keeping terms and conditions fresh (pasting extra information to existing documents rather than cutting them), and other failings often lead to client complaints about the service they received. These complaints can lead to the need to deal with Legal Ombudsman enquiries and, if misconduct is alleged, also the SRA. Perceived poor service can have consequences, be they reputational, word-of-mouth, or poor Google reviews.

The sensible COLP will want to ensure that they have all managers and employees on side with client care initiatives that ensure:

- Client care literature is reviewed and revised on a regular basis. It is poor practice to add information without considering what should be culled.
- That client care literature suits the needs of clients of different departments of the firm. Rarely is it best practice to respond to the duties described in chapter 8 of the Codes with standardised documentation and whilst it is necessary to take the extreme option of writing bespoke literature for individual clients, occasionally this may be appropriate, and always the needs of different types of clients should be considered.
- The requirements to consider a client's needs and attributes (as described in the SRA Codes requirements about service and competence) is taken on board by all fee earners.
- That there is an audit trail to show that each client knows at least the following information, so that they cannot express surprise at what happens during the retainer:
  - Exactly what you will (and won't) be doing.
  - Significant steps along the way.
  - How long the matter should take to complete.
  - The costs involved.
  - The risks.

  - The service standards you will be operating to, including how you intend to communicate with them and how often you will communicate (particularly if the retainer will be long and with legitimate intervals when nothing happens quickly).
  - Complaints handling.
  - SRA regulatory information.
- Some information that is standard – e.g., the regulatory information, information about data protection, financial services etc. – can be added to terms of business documents, but again the content should be accessible and easy for all clients to understand.

It is also important that the COLP and managers do not ignore competencies that support the delivery of these standards. Effective communication – with all staff having the confidence to speak with clients and prospective clients, identify and communicate appropriately with those who may be vulnerable, and also deliver difficult messages or messages to difficult clients – is a good compliance tool.

Finally, the COLP will want to ensure that duties relating to costs information are met. This topic – and any incorrect or ambiguous communications about cost matters – might lead to both the Legal Ombudsman and the SRA having concerns about the firm. Price transparency (and accuracy) must be demonstrated. Is information provided by fee earners consistent with any other publicity about costs generated by the firm? We now have the SRA Transparency Rules, which apply to certain services. Is the website data consistent with information provided by relevant departments? Who is responsible for ensuring the updating and continuing accuracy of website information? Do fee earners (and their supervisors) ensure that costs information is kept updated and, where changes are appropriate, that this is explained to the client?

Suggestions for systems and controls to support effective governance

Development of a client care policy that embodies the firm's values and commitments to client service.

There should be a procedure to ensure the following steps are taken:

- The correct client is identified.
- Other parties are identified, and duties to the underlying client are clarified.

- Client's needs are ascertained.
- Any vulnerability issues are identified.
- The scope of the instructions are described to the client in sufficient detail with major milestones identified.
- Method and frequency of communications are stated.
- Service standards are stated.
- Details of relevant fee earners and supervisors are provided.
- Costs information is clearly stated, and includes an indication of the overall cost, including potential liability for other party costs.
- Complaint and regulatory information is provided.
- Any other information specific to the particular instructions is recorded.

Template client care and terms of business documentation can be (and usually are) used, but the COLP will want to have a review cycle for these to ensure that they remain accurate. Supervisory oversight to ensure that this information remains accurate or has been updated is also best practice.

21. Code provision – Providing services to the public: publicity

Paragraphs 8.8 and 8.9 of the Solicitors' Code, applied in identical form by reference in paragraph 7.1 (c) of the Firm Code, are the publicity duties stated by the SRA. These are as follows:

- *"You ensure that any publicity in relation to your practice is accurate and not misleading, including that relating to your charges and the circumstances in which interest is payable by or to clients.*
- *You do not make unsolicited approaches to members of the public, with the exception of current or former clients, in order to advertise legal services provided by you, or your business or employer."*

Publicity is a defined term. We are told that this reference:

> *"Includes all promotional material and activity, including the name or description of your firm, stationery, advertisements, brochures, websites, directory entries, media appearances, promotional press releases, and direct approaches to potential clients and other persons, whether conducted in person, in writing, or in electronic form, but does not include press releases prepared on behalf of a client."*

Risk management

The SRA's interest in publicity adds to the legal starting point about advertising that applies to all businesses. The regulatory duties impose higher, and more restrictive, standards. It is significant that this is a topic where the SRA has tightened restrictions over the past decade. Its rationale for this position is because of the connection with many of the basic ethical behaviours described in the SRA Principles; poor publicity will compromise Principle 2 (trust and confidence in the profession), Principle 4 (honesty), Principle 5 (integrity), and Principle 7 (acting in each client's best interests).

Publicity extends to every communication with clients about their matters and about the firm and individuals within the firm. It extends to publicity about the firm that is directed at the public at large and prospective clients in particular.

We are prohibited from making unsolicited approaches. Clarification on this can be extracted from the publicity definition, which describes "*direct approaches to potential clients and other persons, whether conducted in person, in writing, or in electronic form*". This is a broad declaration and the SRA has provided further guidance on the meaning[13] in which the SRA has confirmed that targeted approaches to individual members of the public is a breach of the standards.

This must be understood by all managers and employees who may conduct publicity that could generate business, plus anyone involved in marketing, whether they are colleagues or external consultants. With the latter, any activity that they undertake which would be a breach of the duties if undertaken by you, will in fact be considered as a breach by you.

Publicity hotspots need to be managed; for example, have confidentiality and data protection duties been considered, and have duties to the court in particular matters been reconciled with any publicity initiatives?

Suggestions for systems and controls to support effective governance

The COLP will want to be satisfied that managers and employees are clear about the risks of misleading publicity and correct anything that is not correct. Everyone should understand what is meant by unsolicited approaches. The marketing team needs to understand the significance of advertising and publicity in an authorised law firm and work within the restraints imposed in the SRA Codes. An audit should be undertaken of third parties producing marketing and publicity on behalf of the firm, as well as third party referrers, to ensure that none of their activities is in breach of these restrictions.

Other parts of the SRA Standards and Regulations of relevance to the COLP
The COLP is quite justified in concentrating on the Principles and the Codes of Conduct. After all, these apply to everyone and are more likely to be breached or involve high-risk decisions. However, and bearing in mind that the only definite exclusion from the COLP's responsibilities is the SRA Accounts Rules, there is a lot more in the STaRs that must be incorporated into the COLP's risk analysis.

The COLP will want to familiarise themselves with the remainder of the STaRs to understand which other parts are relevant. Not all parts will be, but it is important that the COLP and managers are agreed on the reasons why this may be so and be prepared to justify such a decision to the SRA. Where the other parts of the STaRs are relevant to the firm, the COLP should ensure that there are systems and controls in place to demonstrate effective guidance.

The following is a summary of the other parts presented in alphabetical order:

SRA Application, Notice, Review and Appeal Rules
These are housekeeping Rules intended to regularise the way in which the SRA handles all applications made by individuals and authorised law firms and explaining appeals channels. The COLP may well head up such applications – for example, those relating to colleagues wishing to qualify as a solicitor or be registered as a foreign lawyer – and understanding the correct mechanisms will assist with the smooth completion of such matters.

SRA Assessment of Character and Suitability Rules
These Rules explain the SRA's criteria for deciding whether certain individuals (prospective solicitors, individuals seeking restoration to the roll, European and foreign lawyers in applications for registration or renewal of registration, non-solicitors seeking authorisation as role-holders) have the correct character and suitability for the positions they seek. Sometimes the COLP and other colleagues will be supporting such applications and, in these circumstances, will want to be satisfied that their endorsement is consistent with the criteria in these Rules and supports the SRA fulfil its obligations to regulate in the public interest. In other circumstances, any application made in bad faith might have repercussions for the firm and for these reasons the COLP will want to have influence over applicants and their behaviours.

Authorisation of Firms Rules

Such is the significance of these Rules to the entity and the COLP, they are referenced throughout this book. These are a set of provisions that apply to the SRA's authorisation of law firms. Significantly, for compliance officers, these Rules state the necessity for role-holders as a term of authorisation and the personal attributes required of them. The Rules also set out circumstances in which extra conditions may be applied to authorisation and when authorisation may be withdrawn. The COLP will want to be satisfied that the firm's ability to provide legal services, which is entirely dependent on retaining its authorised status, is not challenged. Matters that are likely to spur the SRA into further enquiries relate of course to risks to client money, which the COFA will want to manage and mitigate, but also more generally will include where there is lack of effective governance or leadership and other circumstances where the compliance culture is poor and has an impact on the wellbeing of managers and employees and the delivery of a proper standard of service to clients.

SRA Authorisation of Individuals Regulations

The SRA's requirements relating to how an individual can qualify and seek admission as a solicitor are here, as well as matters relating to the issue of practising certificates to solicitors and the registration of European lawyers (noting that new registrations are now restricted to Swiss lawyers for Brexit-related reasons) and the registration of foreign lawyers. The Regulations also state what authorisation (i.e., the granting of a practising certificate etc.) entitles the authorised individual to do. The COLP will want to be satisfied that they understand admission requirements and practising rights. Knowledge of these regulations will also be relevant to any colleague involved in the training of individuals seeking qualification as a solicitor, anyone involved in the SRA annual renewal exercise, and HR colleagues. Where this individual is not also the COLP, the latter will want to have confidence that there is an appropriate engagement with the training requirements.

SRA Education, Training and Assessment Provider Regulations

In circumstances where the firm continues to offer training contracts (which, it should be noted, will be phased out completely by 2032 and is currently running alongside the replacement Solicitors Qualifying Examination route to admission), the COLP will want reassurance that there is compliance with these Regulations. This will be obtained from the firm's managers, the training principal, and HR colleagues.

SRA Financial Services (Scope) Rules and the SRA Financial Services (Conduct of Business) Rules

A compliance decision that the COLP must not swerve concerns financial services and whether the firm delivers financial services to any of its clients. This is because there are strict legal restrictions on the provision of financial services (through the Financial Services and Markets Act 2000 and related legislation) and regulatory controls imposed on the majority of financial businesses and providers (through the Prudential Regulation Authority and the Financial Conduct Authority).

Solicitors employed in SRA-authorised law firms (and other managers and employees) are entitled to perform a limited range of financial services known as exempt regulated activities under the supervision of the SRA and subject to compliance with the SRA's rules. The Scope Rules describe the extent of the exemption including conditions which attach to some services. The Conduct of Business Rules explain how the services must be delivered.

The COLP must understand whether the firm is providing exempt regulated activities and whether the requirements of both the Scope Rules and the Conduct of Business Rules are being satisfied. Failure to comply with these sets of Rules is likely to be both a regulatory breach and a legal issue as the firm may be providing a financial service in breach of the strict controls in the legislation.

The COLP will want to have answers to the following questions:

- Which departments are delivering exempt regulated activities to clients?
- What are the financial products and are we meeting any conditions attached to them?
- For example, are we performing what is described as insurance distribution activities, which trigger a number of compliance requirements including registration on the FCA's Financial Services Register, the internal appointment of an insurance distribution officer who has specific statutory duties, a specific status disclosure statement that must be provided to clients where relevant, training of staff, and the maintenance of particular records?
- More generally, do staff need training on this topic?
- Are we keeping the required records?
- Are we acting in each client's best interests when we deliver these services? Do we have competence? Do we consider each client's needs?

SRA Overseas and Cross-border Practice Rules

The COLP must decide whether these Rules are relevant to the firm's circumstances. Overseas for regulatory purposes means anywhere in the world outside England and Wales.

The COLP will want to consider whether the domestic regulated entity has an overseas practice. This triggers regulatory duties, which includes a proportionate risk management oversight of that practice and certain notification requirements. This is discussed in more detail in chapter seven.

SRA Regulatory and Disciplinary Procedure Rules

These Rules are part of the COLP's knowledge bank, providing the roleholder with essential information about SRA enforcement work, and the range of sanctions and controls that can be used against defaulting solicitors, RELS, RFLS, authorised firms, and everyone who works in these firms.

SRA Statutory Trust Rules

Another section that should be filed in the COLP's knowledge bank, but hopefully not need to read. These Rules state the SRA's powers in respect of monies which it ceases as part of an intervention into a practice.

SRA Roll, Registers and Publication Regulations

Solicitor records are stated to be on the roll of solicitors maintained by the SRA. The SRA also maintains registers of European lawyers, foreign lawyers, and authorised bodies. Information about these categories is in the public domain. The COLP will want to ensure that the information is accurate, hence the need to ensure that reporting and notifications duties are working satisfactorily.

SRA Transparency Rules

This is an important part of the STaRs. The COLP must be confident that there is full compliance with this set of Rules. It is important because it supports the SRA in its regulatory objectives, which are consumer-facing and respond to the duty to enable competition in the marketplace. The Rules are designed to ensure that consumers, particularly prospective and current clients, have access to information that allows them to make informed choices. Some elements apply to firms if they provide certain types of legal services to certain types of clients, whilst other parts apply to all firms. The SRA regularly checks law firm websites and challenges firms to demonstrate compliance.

Sense-testing questions that the COLP should consider include:

- Do we publicise the fact that we deliver the services listed in the SRA Transparency Rules?
- If it is necessary to publish costs information, and are we doing this in a way that is clear, accessible, and accurate?
- Do we provide up to date information about the experience and qualifications of all relevant staff (including supervisors)?
- Do we comply with the mandatory duty to publish complaints information, and is this information also presented in a clear and easy to read style?
- Are we confident that colleagues in departments that provide services subject to costs publicity understand the significance of the Transparency Rules?
- Is the pricing structure applied in practice consistent with the information published on the website?
- Generally, are individuals monitoring costs information and providing updates to clients about changes to original quotes etc?

SRA Indemnity (Enactment) Rules 2012, Indemnity Rules 2012, and SRA Indemnity Insurance Rules

It is an important consumer protection, and a regulatory requirement, that authorised law firms have professional indemnity insurance that meets minimum conditions prescribed in the SRA Indemnity Insurance Rules. An authorised law firm without correct insurance is unable to continue to provide legal services. The COLP will want to be satisfied on the indemnity position and should bear in mind that insurers are increasingly interested in compliance data and risk and compliance procedures that are in operation.

The SRA Indemnity Rules 2012[14] are less likely to be relevant, but for the sake of completeness the COLP should know that they apply to the Solicitors Indemnity Fund (SIF), which applied to the previous regime, and run-off cover that is available in some specific circumstances. This run-off cover is soon to end as it is intended that the SIF will be closed.

SRA Compensation Fund Rules 2021

The COLP will also want to add this information to their knowledge bank. This Fund is sometimes described as the fund of last resort, and offers compensatory payments in certain conditions to individuals and certain other types of entity who have suffered loss because of a defaulting practitioner.

SRA Glossary

The COLP will find it useful to know that the SRA assigns defined meanings to certain words and phrases in the STaRs. These are italicised in the text and the meaning is provided in the Glossary section.

References

1 www.sra.org.uk/solicitors/standards-regulations/authorisation-firms-rules/
2 www.sra.org.uk/solicitors/guidance/authorisation-approval-role-holders/
3 The archived Handbook is available at www.sra.org.uk/solicitors/handbook/
4 www.sra.org.uk/solicitors/standards-regulations/code-conduct-firms/
5 The SRA's approach to equality, diversity and inclusion (November 2019), www.sra.org.uk/solicitors/guidance/sra-approach-equality-diversity-inclusion/
Warning Notice: Offensive Communications (November 2019), www.sra.org.uk/solicitors/guidance/offensive-communications/
Workplace Environment: risks of failing to protect and support colleagues (February 2022), www.sra.org.uk/solicitors/guidance/workplace-environment/
6 According to the SRA glossary, Client means the person for whom you act and, where the context permits, includes prospective and former clients in the SRA Financial Services (Scope) Rules, in relation to any regulated financial services activities carried on by an authorised body for a trust or the estate of a deceased person (including a controlled trust), means the trustees or personal representatives in their capacity as such and not any person who is a beneficiary under the trust or interested in the estate.
7 www.sra.org.uk/solicitors/guidance/prohibition-of-referral-fees-in-laspo-56-60/
8 www.sra.org.uk/solicitors/guidance/putting-matters-right-own-interest-conflicts/
9 According to the SRA glossary, a Relevant insolvency event occurs in relation to a body if:
   a) A resolution for a voluntary winding up of the body is passed without a declaration of solvency under section 89 of the Insolvency Act 1986;
   b) The body enters administration within the meaning of paragraph 1(2)(b) of Schedule B1 to that Act;
   c) An administrative receiver within the meaning of section 251 of that Act is appointed;
   d) A meeting of creditors is held in relation to the body under section 95 of that Act (creditors' meeting which has the effect of converting a members' voluntary winding up into a creditors' voluntary winding up);

e) An order for the winding up of the body is made;
f) All of the managers in a body which is unincorporated have been adjudicated bankrupt; or
g) The body is an overseas company or a societas Europaea registered outside England, Wales, Scotland and Northern Ireland and the body is subject to an event in its country of incorporation analogous to an event as set out in paragraphs (a) to (f) above;

Occurs in relation to an individual if:

- The individual is adjudged bankrupt;
- A debt relief order has been made under Part 7A of the Insolvency Act 1986 in respect of that individual; or
- The individual has entered into an individual voluntary arrangement or a partnership voluntary arrangement under the Insolvency Act 1986.

10 According to the SRA glossary, Register includes:

- The roll and the register of solicitors with practising certificates kept under Part I of the SA;
- The register of European lawyers;
- The register of foreign lawyers; and
- The register of authorised bodies kept under the AJA and the LSA.

11 https://legalservicesboard.org.uk

12 www.sra.org.uk/solicitors/guidance/identifying-client/

13 www.sra.org.uk/solicitors/guidance/unsolicited-approaches-advertising/

14 www.sra.org.uk/solicitors/standards-regulations/indemnity-rules-2012/

Chapter 5: The COFA's essential knowledge and suggested systems and controls

We have now considered the essential regulatory knowledge required by the COLP and made suggestions as to systems and controls that may usefully be deployed to manage the risk of breaches or non-compliance.

A similar exercise should be undertaken in respect of the COFA role.

We have already discussed that the firm will be taking a risk if it puts forward for approval (deemed approval or otherwise) a COFA who has little, or inadequate, knowledge of those parts of the STaRs that are addressed to them personally. Put bluntly, this lack of knowledge may mean that the SRA is reluctant to approve or allow the appointment.

The extent of the COFA's responsibilities contrasted with the role of the COLP and the role of the firm's managers

The observations expressed in chapter four apply equally here and in respect of the COFA role. It is a condition of authorisation that all authorised law firms have a COFA. The COFA need not be a lawyer but must be a manager or employee of the firm.

The COFA has the personal duties described in paragraph 9.2 of the SRA Code of Conduct for Firms:

> *"If you are a COFA you must take all reasonable steps to:*
> 1. *Ensure that your firm and its managers and employees comply with any obligations imposed upon them under the SRA Accounts Rules;*
> 2. *Ensure that a prompt report is made to the SRA of any facts or matters that you reasonably believe are capable of amounting to a serious breach of the SRA Accounts Rules which apply to them;*
> 3. *Notwithstanding sub-paragraph (b), you ensure that the SRA is informed promptly of any facts or matters that you reasonably believe should be brought to its attention in order that it may investigate whether a serious breach of its regulatory arrangements has occurred or otherwise exercise its regulatory powers."*

This does not transfer exclusive responsibility for all compliance matters relating to the subject area to the COFA. As with the COLP, there is an expectation of collective sharing of compliance governance with the firm's managers (who are told as much in chapter eight of the SRA Code of Conduct for Firms) and also by the directional instruction at paragraph 2.1 (c) that the firm (i.e., the managers/owners of the authorised entity) put in place systems to ensure *"your compliance officers are able to discharge their duties under paragraphs 9.1 and 9.2"*. Any compliance officer who does not receive full support is best advised to consider whether they wish to continue in their designated role.

However, regardless of this support, the COFA will want to be confident that they have certain personal knowledge and skills with which to fulfil their role.

Case study

In 2019, a law firm partner who was the COFA was fined £10,000 by the Solicitors Disciplinary Tribunal, and ordered to pay costs of just under £8,000, in connection with failings connected with Accounts Rules issues. These included not knowing that qualified accountants' reports had to be filed with the SRA and not knowing about the need to carry out reconciliations. The SDT found that the breaches had been caused by naivety and carelessness, but nevertheless these were examples of "manifest incompetence".

Key knowledge from the SRA Standards and Regulations of relevance to the COFA

A COFA who focuses exclusively on the SRA Accounts Rules and does not consider the relevance of other parts of the STaRs is doing themselves and the firm a disservice.

The SRA has a regulatory duty to protect clients and the public and this includes the protection of client money, and for these reasons the COFA needs to understand not only the Accounts Rules but also the wider regulatory position regarding risks and risk management described elsewhere in the rulebook.

Relevant sections are described below.

SRA Principles

In contrast to many other businesses that operate accounts for the deposit of other people's money, and/or otherwise handle large sums of other people's money, law firms are not directly regulated by the financial services industry in order to be able to do this. However, without proper controls, our right to do this could easily be challenged by those who champion consumer protection.

The simple fact is that most clients trust us with their money, and that in the majority of matters there is no reason to suggest that this trust is misplaced. Much of this is tied up with our adherence to the high standards of behaviour described in the SRA Principles. As with the COLP, these are the first calling point for the firm's COFA. The COFA will want to understand the relationship between the Principles and client money protection.

The current seven Principles do not specifically make mention of client money. However, for the duration of the SRA Handbook (2011-2019) there was a discrete principle to deal with the point; the now archived Principle 10 of the SRA Handbook stated that "*you must protect client money and assets*" with accompanying guidance that added "*This Principle goes to the heart of the duty to act in the best interests of your clients. You should play your part in, e.g., protecting money, documents or other property belonging to your clients which has been entrusted to you or your firm.*"

No doubt this was delivering a message not only to solicitors and authorised law firms, but also to the Legal Services Board and all other interested stakeholders, that the SRA was truly a risk-based and new-style regulator that could be trusted to address the big risk topics.

This headline Principle did not survive the review that led to the introduction of the STaRs, but nevertheless the Principles that we have applied since 2019 all implicitly support the duty to protect client money and the more general consumer protection objectives described in section 1 of the Legal Services Act. Consider the table overleaf.

Table 3: Principles and behaviours breaching them.

Principle	Examples of behaviours involving money which would demonstrate a breach of the Principle
Principle 1 – You act in a way that upholds the constitutional principle of the rule of law, and the proper administration of justice.	Bringing unarguable cases before the courts at cost to the client concerned. Committing an act of theft or fraud involving money.
Principle 2 – You act in a way that upholds public trust and confidence in the solicitor's profession and in legal services provided by authorised persons.	Having a connection with dubious investment schemes, which causes, amongst other things, financial harm to the investors. Misuse of your client account as a way to shelter or hide money (as may be the case with insolvency proceedings, acting on instructions that may have a link with tax avoidance or evasion motives etc.).
Principle 3 – You act with independence.	Relationships with non-clients that have a detrimental impact on dealings with clients and the protection of their money.
Principle 4 – You act with honesty.	Stealing client money. Committing a fraud on your client. Not telling the truth to your client about their money.
Principle 5 – You act with integrity.	Delaying the payment of disbursements when in receipt of client funds. Making improper payments out of client account. Failing to protect clients from mortgage fraud. Not being open in your dealings with the client.
Principle 6 – You act in a way that encourages equality, diversity, and inclusion.	Taking advantage of a client's vulnerabilities.
Principle 7 – You act in the best interests of each client.	Not protecting confidential information and thereby not protecting client money. Acting without due competence and putting client money at risk. Not communicating with a client in a clear way about client money issues.

Case study

In 2022, a solicitor was jailed for stealing the assets of a client who was suffering from dementia. The SRA investigated the solicitor, and his client account and other financial transactions, and referred the misconduct to the SDT. The SDT decided that the solicitor should be struck off the roll. The SDT commented that misconduct did not get much worse than what they had seen in respect of this solicitor's behaviour.

SRA Codes of Conduct

Whilst it is the case that the majority of the content of these Codes is applied to the provision of legal services of a suitable quality and with a demonstration of professionalism, and will consequently be predominantly the COLP's domain, there is content that is relevant to the COFA's role.

Consider the referenced sections below.

Maintaining trust and acting fairly

The Solicitors' Code and Firm Code each have an identical duty at Paragraph 1.2 that states, "*You do not abuse your position by taking unfair advantage of clients or others*". This arises because of the nature of the solicitor–client relationship and the information asymmetry that usually exists between the two sides. Anything we may do that does not take account of the needs of the client might well be construed as taking unfair advantage. This will extend to the handling of client money.

Compliance and business systems

Paragraph 2.4 of the Firm Code states that, "*You actively monitor your financial stability and business viability. Once you are aware that you will cease to operate, you effect the orderly wind-down of your activities.*" Financial instability and lack of business viability are seen as potential threats to client money protection. The duty to monitor these issues are addressed to the firm itself – i.e., the managers – but compliance officers will be expected to report issues promptly to the SRA. It will be sensible for the COLP and COFA to discuss coverage of this, and arguably better practice for this to come within the COFA's portfolio.

Cooperation and accountability

Chapter three of the Firm Code addresses the managers of the firm and requires them to notify the SRA of certain matters including the following:

- *"Indicators of serious financial difficulty relating to you;*
- *If a relevant insolvency event occurs in relation to you;*

If you intend to, or become aware that you will, cease operating as a legal business."

Again, financial insecurities that arise in connection with the firm, and decisions to close, are of interest to the SRA, which will want to have confidence that these matters do not compromise the protection of client money. It would be sensible for this to be the COFA' s reporting responsibility.

Service and competence

The Solicitors' Code, paragraph 3.1 and Firm Code, paragraph 4.1 say:

> *"You only act for clients on instructions from the client, or from someone properly authorised to provide instructions on their behalf. If you have reason to suspect that the instructions do not represent your client's wishes, you do not act unless you have satisfied yourself that they do. However, in circumstances where you have legal authority to act notwithstanding that it is not possible to obtain or ascertain the instructions of your client, then you are subject to the overriding obligation to protect your client's best interests."*

We act as our client's agent and must ensure that our actions are justifiable on the basis that we have been instructed to do or not do something. This extends to matters relating to client money.

Service and competence – supervision and managerial responsibilities

The Solicitors' Code imposes personal duties on solicitors, RELs, and RFLs who supervise or manage others. These duties are in paragraphs 3.5 and 3.6 and extend to the supervisor remaining accountable for work carried out by those they supervise and ensuring that they are competent and, amongst other things, keep their understanding of ethical and regulatory obligations up to date. There are overlapping duties on the managers/owners of the authorised law firm in the Firm Code.

Proper service standards and competency must be displayed in all our dealings for and on behalf of clients, and this extends to dealings with client money. Supervisory and managerial oversight must extend to this topic, and supervisors have an important compliance role in supporting the COFA by providing feedback on any breaches, training needs or similar.

Client money and assets

Chapter four of the Solicitors' Code and Chapter five of the Firm Code contain the identically worded duties, *"You properly account to clients for any financial benefit*[1] *you receive as a result of their instructions, except where they have agreed otherwise,"* and *"You safeguard money and assets entrusted to you by clients and others"*.

In many ways this is the current home of the client money principle, which was previously in the SRA Handbook (2011-2019). The duties in both Codes apply to everyone in the firm, regardless of position or experience.

Client information – costs

We have the following duties:

> *"You ensure that clients receive the best possible information about how their matter will be priced and, both at the time of engagement and when appropriate as their matter progresses, about the likely overall cost of the matter and any costs incurred."*

> *"You ensure that any publicity in relation to your practice is accurate and not misleading, including that relating to your charges and the circumstances in which interest is payable by or to clients."*

Protecting client money requires effective communication, as demonstrated by these client duties.

SRA Accounts Rules

One of the SRA's regulatory objectives is consumer protection and the safeguarding of client money is a risk priority. We are expected to manage this risk through compliance with the SRA Accounts Rules, which are in the STaRs.

There is absolutely no ambiguity about who has responsibilities, together with the managers, for this set of Rules. The clues are hiding in clear sight in both the COFA title and in the detail of paragraph 9.2 of the SRA Code of Conduct for Firms. The SRA will expect nothing less than a comprehensive knowledge of the Accounts Rules on the part of the incumbent COFA.

The Accounts Rules included in the STaRs are very different in size and format from the equivalent rules they replaced. Some practitioners might recall the previous version, the Solicitors Accounts Rules 2011, which were very long and copiously exacting in style. In fact, the SRA had largely adopted the Accounts Rules response of its own predecessor (the Law Society of England and Wales) and cut and pasted huge swathes of its requirements as its own response. This was an unsatisfactory response for a new style regulator, and it made amends in 2019 with its own quite radical format. COFAs now have a slimline and often very outcomes-focused style of Accounts Rules with which to ensure client money is safe.

The introduction to these Rules tells us that the Rules apply to the managers of authorised law firms and everyone, regardless of who they are or what they do, who work in the firm. This is confirmed in the application section of the Rules, which also repeats the message stated elsewhere in the STaRs, that the firm's managers are jointly and severally responsible for compliance by the firm, its managers, and employees. We are also told that firms will need systems and controls that must be appropriate to the nature and volumes of client transactions being dealt with and the amount of client money held or received.

The content of the Accounts Rules is shown below, together with a commentary on risk issues and suggested systems and controls.

1. Rule provision – Client money definition

Rule 2 of the SRA Accounts Rules provides the definition of client money as money held or received by the authorised law in the following circumstances:

- Money relating to regulated services delivered by the firm to a client;
- On behalf of a third party in respect of the regulated services you deliver;
- Money you hold as a trustee or in some other office-holder role (e.g., as an attorney, Court of Protection deputy, etc.); and
- Money received in respect of your fees and any unpaid disbursements, if held prior to delivery of a bill for the same.

This is useful and is in itself defined content, but also includes defined phrases within it that must be noted:

- Regulated services means the legal and other professional services that the business offers and that are regulated by the SRA.
- Fees means your own charges or profit costs (including VAT where relevant).
- Disbursements means any costs or expenses paid or to be paid to a third party on behalf of the client or trust (including VAT where relevant). This definition does not include office expenses.

Risk management

As with many similar regulatory and professional duties, it is vital that everyone understands what is and isn't defined as client money.

Misunderstanding this concept means that the correct application of other Accounts Rules requirements is more likely to be haphazard.

Some common misunderstandings that can arise include the mistreatment of monies received from third parties in terms expressed as acting as agent or stakeholder or monies to be held to the sender's order. These are all examples of client money.

Money received in advance of the provision of services, or received in anticipation of disbursements not yet incurred, should be treated as money on account of costs. These sums are also client money unless the firm is able to rely on a very specific and narrow exception as described in rule 2.2.

Suggestions for systems and controls to support effective governance

Training of fee earners about types of client money is important, otherwise there may be misunderstandings and incorrect conversations with clients, with third parties and the SRA.

2. Rule provision – Money on account of costs

Rule 2.2 states that if the only client money held by the firm relates to your unbilled fees and disbursements for which you are liable, and you have no other reason to maintain a client account, then this money does not need to be paid into a client account.

This is subject to a pre-condition that the client is told of this in advance. If this exception is used then the following requirements do not apply:

- Obligations relating to the use of client account.
- Instant access to the monies.
- The duty to keep client money separate from the firm's money.
- Interest provisions.
- Accounting record-keeping requirements, which dictate that a list of all the balances is maintained showing the client ledger records and having a cash book showing a running total of all transactions through the client account.
- Obtaining and delivery of an accountant's report.

Risk management

This carve-out from the default duty to hold client money in a client account was an interesting innovation in the Accounts Rules launched in 2019.

This seems like a light touch move, and it certainly does reduce the need to comply with other parts of the Accounts Rules, but it is certainly not a risk-free decision. Overall, you will need to be confident that this decision can be reconciled with Principles such as trust and confidence, integrity, and acting in each client's best interests, and the Codes duty to safeguard client money.

Whilst Accounts Rules record-keeping might be reduced, this might mean that there needs to be more careful financial management so that the clients' monies are not put at risk, that the arrangement does not mean that you are putting your interests in front of your clients (i.e., an own interest conflict), that any repayments can be made, and that the funds are protected notwithstanding the closure of the firm or any insolvency event occurs.

It will also be necessary to consider whether clients are given information in a way that is clear. The Rules do not require us to seek informed consent (as is the case when other exceptions are being sought) but nonetheless we need to be able to demonstrate that we have effectively communicated our decision to our client base and the implications should the firm face financial difficulties. For example, unlike monies held in a client account, money held in this way is not ringfenced and in the event of the firm's insolvency, could become part of the insolvent estate.

Suggestions for systems and controls to support effective governance

The firm's managers must make a decision about whether it is possible, and, as importantly, desirable, to make use of this exemption. An incorrect decision will be a serious breach of the Accounts Rules.

If it is used, compliance will be supported by training of staff so that they can support clients in their understanding of how their money will be held.

The firm's client care documentation should include information about this.

3. Rule provision – Client accounts

Except in the circumstances and carve-out described above, client money must be paid promptly into a client account in accordance with Rule 2.3. This is subject to the following exceptions:

- If money is held in accordance with a role as trustee, attorney, deputy etc. and placing money in a client account would create a conflict with obligations that arise as a consequence of your appointment.

- The client money is a payment received from the Legal Aid Agency in respect of your costs.
- You agree an alternative arrangement with an individual client/third party for whom the money is held, provided that this arrangement is evidenced in writing.

Again, it is important to ensure that defined terms are understood, such as "Client account", which is defined in Rule 3 (see below) and "Costs", which mean your fees and disbursements.

Risk management

This clause also shows a change of approach from the regulator, who has moved away from mandatory timekeeping requirements to a position where the firm is expected to consider what is prompt and ensure that this decision is justifiable and consistently adopted. Previously, firms were required to place client monies in to a client account "without delay", a seemingly vague phrase with a surprisingly exact meaning of the day of receipt or by the end of the next working day. Anecdotally, many firms now have arrangements to make payments into client accounts in 48 hours or 72 hours etc. Whatever is agreed, it is important that the COFA has evidence that this is realistic and is achieved.

Legal aid agency money can be paid immediately into the firm's business account.

Alternative arrangements must be managed carefully with appropriate evidence that this is in the client's best interests.

Suggestions for systems and controls to support effective governance

Monitoring of banks and building societies should be undertaken to ensure that there are not any inadvertent breaches of this Rule such as might arise in circumstances where the title of the account is incorrect or similar.

4. Rule provision – Access to client money

Rule 2.4 provides for availability of client money on demand unless an alternative arrangement is agreed with the client/third party for whom the money is held, and the arrangement is in writing.

Risk management

On demand means instant access to client money. This is an important concept in terms of the safeguarding of client money, in terms of trust and confidence, and when considering the duty to act in each client's best interests.

In practice, instant access means that client money should be accessible without delay.

This client protection means that alternative arrangements place the firm in a higher risk position and the COFA will want to be satisfied that the decision can be justified and must only be executed with an individual client's informed consent.

Suggestions for systems and controls to support effective governance

Monitoring of the conditions that apply to the firm's client account(s) is advised. Where an alternative agreement is arranged, the arrangement must be in writing and with an explanation of the consequences of non-instant access. A template letter might be appropriate.

5. Rule provision – Return of client money

Rule 2.5 deals with circumstances when it is no longer necessary for the firm to hold client money: "*You ensure that client money is returned promptly to the client, or the third party for whom the money is held, as soon as there is no longer any proper reason to hold those funds*".

Risk management

The COFA must be confident that there is a process to ensure the prompt return of monies. Again, as we now are provided with the adjective "prompt" and not a specific time limit, the firm must set its own timeline, but "almost immediately after the transaction is completed/the firm's involvement is at an end" seems a sensible consideration.

Running alongside this objective is the need to consider the restraints on the destination of returned monies. Surplus funds – monies that are not to be used to settle obligations arising strictly in connection with the transaction – must be returned to the client or the paying third party in order to avoid a breach of the banking prohibition in Rule 3.3.

Suggestions for systems and controls to support effective governance

The firm should have an agreed procedure for file closure that includes time requirements with appropriate supervisory and accounts team oversight of compliance.

6. Rule provision – Client account conditions

Rule 3 states conditions attached to the type of account in which client money must be held. These are described in Rules 3.1 and 3.2 as follows:

> *"The client account must be held at a branch (or the head office) of a bank or building society in England and Wales."*

The name of the client account must include the name of the authorised body and the word "client".

Risk management

Except in the circumstances described in Rule 2.1(d), so that the only client money that the firm receives is advance payments for fees and unpaid disbursements, then client money must be paid into a client account promptly.

The COFA must be satisfied that the type and style of client account completely complies with the Rule 3 requirements. This is because placing client money into this type of account ringfences it in the event of a law firm's insolvency or other financial issues. UK banks or building societies are regulated by the Prudential Regulation Authority and monies deposited with them are protected by the Financial Services Compensation Scheme.

There are two types of client account – separate designated client accounts (i.e., accounts for money relating to a single client) and general client accounts (i.e., accounts where the money of more than one client is pooled).

Suggestions for systems and controls to support effective governance

It would be prudent to monitor the banks and building societies in which client monies are held.

7. Rule provision – Use of the client account and the banking prohibition

Rule 3.3 is as follows:

> *"You must not use a client account to provide banking facilities to clients or third parties. Payments into, and transfers or withdrawals from a client account must be in respect of the delivery by you of regulated services."*

The meaning of the reference to client account is described elsewhere in parts of Rule 2 of the SRA Accounts Rules. Regulated services is a defined phrase meaning the legal and professional services that you provide that are regulated by the SRA and includes, where appropriate, acting as a trustee or as the holder of a specified office or appointment.

Risk management

The COFA must understand the meaning of this banking prohibition and have confidence that the client account is not being used for such purposes. This will be achieved only with strict controls, empowering accounts and finance colleagues to be able to challenge payments into, transfers, or withdrawals, and with other colleagues understanding the limited access to client accounts that they can offer clients and third parties. It is also necessary to consider what practical steps can be taken to limit the sharing of client account details with clients and third parties outside the firm.

The SRA has issued two warning notices on the improper use of the firm's client account, numerous case studies, and taken account of relevant case law in order to develop its response to the risks associated with the improper use of a firm's client account.

To paraphrase the SRA and case law findings, use of the client account as a banking facility is objectionable in itself (with the point being that we are not regulated as banking institutions), it increases the risks that the firm will be used for money laundering, and it may be a way for clients to protect their money in insolvency situations.

The SRA has gone on record as saying that a breach of rule 3.3 is a serious matter. Severe sanctions should be expected, particularly because the breach may also mean that there are concerns about non-compliance with Principle 1 (upholding the rule of law), Principle 2 (trust and confidence), Principle 3 (independence), and Principle 5 (integrity).

Case study

In 2022, a partner in a law firm was fined £2,000 by the SRA, and ordered to pay costs of £1,350, after he had allowed charitable trusts to use his firm's client account as a bank whilst they were in the process of opening their own bank accounts. This was held to be a breach of the banking prohibition as contained in the Accounts Rules.

Suggestions for systems and controls to support effective governance

Training of all relevant staff on the banking prohibition and support to ensure effective communication with clients and third parties so that improper instructions are rejected are sensible measures to implement. Training on this topic can also be covered as part of the anti-money laundering response.

Regular reminders of the prohibition can be shared with staff through the use of the many disciplinary decisions in this area. Supervisory oversight can be used to ensure compliance.

8. Rule provision – Client money must be kept separate from non-client money

Rule 4 states the duty to keep client money separate, so that Rule 4.1 describes the duty to separate it from the firm's own money and Rule 4.2 requires you to ensure that funds from mixed payments are allocated to the correct client or business account promptly.

We have already seen that the term "client account" is defined in rules 2 and 3.

"Mixed payments" is also a defined phrase, meaning a payment that includes both client money and non-client money.

Client money is defined in Rule 2. Business account is not defined and is an expression introduced into our vocabulary with the introduction of the STaRs in 2019. However, it can be taken to mean your office account (noting that this term is no longer used by the SRA but continues to be used by many law firms).

Risk management

This should be a familiar concept to the COFA and colleagues in the firm.

"Promptly" has replaced the specific time requirements contained in the previous versions of the Accounts Rules (i.e., the "14-day rule" for the placing of client monies into a client account). This means that the COFA will want to be satisfied that the firm's replacement is justifiable and is in fact prompt, and that the firm's internal systems and controls enable the timing decision to be fulfilled. The SRA is entitled to challenge the firm on decisions made about this and whether there is compliance in practice.

Suggestions for systems and controls to support effective governance

Agreement about the exact meaning of "promptly" that will be applied and a procedure to explain the timing requirements.

9. Rule provision – client money and paying costs

Rule 4.3 deals with payment of the firm's costs from client money held by the firm, imposing the following conditions that apply to its use for this purpose:

- *You must give a bill of costs, or other written notification of the costs incurred, to the client or the paying party;*

- *This must be done before you transfer any client money from a client account to make the payment; and*
- *Any such payment must be for the specific sum identified in the bill of costs, or other written notification of the costs incurred, and covered by the amount held for the particular client or third party.*

"Costs" is defined as meaning the firm's fees and disbursements. "Fees" mean your own charges or profit costs (including any VAT element) and "disbursements" means any costs or expenses paid or to be paid to a third party on behalf of the client or trust (including any VAT element) save for office expenses such as postage and courier fees.

Risk management

The COFA must be satisfied that all conditions are met before monies are transferred from the client account for these purposes. The SRA has issued guidance to support our understanding of its expectations,[2] which provides cautionary commentary in terms of billing in advance for costs and transferring money for costs incurred (either during the relationship or when the matter has been completed).

The SRA's priority is client protection in such circumstances. The COFA will want to be satisfied that nothing about such a transfer challenges items such as the SRA Principles relating to trust and confidence, honesty, integrity, and the duty to act in the best interests of each client. It also is concerned with our compliance with duty expressed in identical form in each of the SRA Codes that we safeguard client money.

Suggestions for systems and controls to support effective governance

Training staff about effective communication with clients and the firm's expectations about the information that must be provided before money on account of costs can be used for costs is sensible, as is appropriate supervisory oversight.

10. Rule provision – Withdrawals from client account

Withdrawals must be made in strict compliance with Rule 5, which states at 5.1 that you only withdraw client money from a client account for the purpose for which it is held or following receipt of instructions from the client or the third party for whom the money is held or on the SRA's written authority or in prescribed circumstances.

Risk management

Knowing that the SRA has a highly restrictive no-banking requirement, it makes sense that the COFA is ensured that there is strict control over withdrawals. Withdrawals will be proper only in the circumstances described here.

All COFAs will be aware that there are sometimes occasion when surplus funds remain in client account and cannot be returned to the legitimate owner (either the client or a third party). In these circumstances, the firm should have a system to deal with the removal of a client account. Self-certification and withdrawal is allowed in very controlled circumstances for sums under £500. For sums over £500, application must be made to the SRA. The COFA should understand that whilst this is a helpful mechanism, it is also an indication that systems and controls have been ineffective in accounting properly to the client/third party. This might indicate systemic failures.

There is not a prescribed timekeeping requirement attached to this requirement but it would be sensible to consider and apply a firmwide requirement relating to the word "prompt".

Suggestions for systems and controls to support effective governance

It is good practice to implement a system that includes the designation of approved signatories and a process for evidencing their authority to withdraw client monies. It will be best practice for the signatories to understand why a withdrawal is requested.

File closure procedures that are designed to ensure the prompt withdrawal of surplus funds will be helpful, as will a procedure for recording monies held for undertakings/retained sums etc., both by accounts teams and the fee earner. Diary maintenance by the fee earner should ensure vigilance over these monies.

Records of self-authorised withdrawals is sensible. Monitoring of these records, plus monitoring of client bills, will ensure that there is staff observance of the firm's procedures, and no unethical practices (such as dummy bills or similar) etc.

11. Rule provision – Withdrawals from client accounts: more requirements

Rule 5.2 requires you – here meaning the firm and its managers – to appropriately authorise and supervise all withdrawals from a client account.

Rule 5.3 states that you – again the firm and managers – should withdraw client money only in circumstances in which sufficient funds are held on behalf of the specific client or third party.

Risk management

Systems and controls must ensure client protection, so of course there must be tight management of withdrawals, bearing in mind the consequences if there is too relaxed an approach. Note the wording refers to both authority and supervision. Many firms insist on double signatures for client account withdrawals, or senior and/or manager signatories, or manager/COFA sign-off. How to comply with Rule 5.2 is not prescribed but the COFA and managers will want to have confidence that their response acts as a safeguard.

Similarly, rule 5.3 requires safeguards to be put in place. Whilst many clients' monies are pooled together in a general account, this is not a common fund and the firm must be satisfied that when withdrawals are made for a specific client that this is with money that is held for that specific client. This requires both good book-keeping and good managerial oversight.

Suggestions for systems and controls to support effective governance

The system for appropriate authorisation as described above is a sensible control. It is important that the COFA has confidence in authorised signatories with appropriate knowledge of the Accounts Rules.

Accounting records that ensure client ledgers are checked before withdrawals are completed and a system for the transfer of costs from a client to your business accounts also help.

12. Rule provision – Correcting breaches

You must correct any breaches of these rules promptly upon discovery. Any money improperly withheld or withdrawn from a client account must be immediately paid into the account or replaced as appropriate.

Risk management

The COFA must have confidence that the firm's systems and controls are sufficient to ensure breaches (accidental and deliberate) are identified and remedied promptly. Client account shortfalls must be corrected immediately. "Promptly" and "immediately" are not defined terms but the sense is clear. The SRA requires the client account to be correct and, if necessary, managers will be required to immediately replace any shortfalls. This is an important duty for managers to understand and ensure that there are resources to cover such an issue. Should serious breaches be reported to the SRA by the COFA, this will be part of the report that must be provided to the SRA.

Suggestions for systems and controls to support effective governance

Rigorous controls over client account, regular reconciliations, and the maintenance of an accurate breaches register will be useful.

In addition, managers should be trained to ensure that this duty, and the possibility that they may be called upon to remedy breaches, is understood.

13. Rule provision – Interest payments

Duties are described in Rule 7. Ordinarily, you (the firm and its managers) must account to clients or third parties for a fair sum of interest on any client money held on their behalf.

In individual circumstances, you may by a written agreement come to a different arrangement but you must provide sufficient information so that the client/third party for whom the money is held provides sufficient information to enable them to give informed consent.

Interest is defined as meaning a fair sum in lieu of interest.

Risk management

The description of a fair sum means that the COFA and managers have important decisions to make about what might be fair and in what circumstances interest will be paid. In order to ensure a consistent approach, many firms have a written interest policy and terms in their client care/terms of business documentation to explain the firm's position.

Carve-outs must be specific to individual clients with the onus on the firm to ensure that there is written evidence of that client's agreement and that the client understands what they are agreeing to give up.

Suggestions for systems and controls to support effective governance

A written interest policy is advisable to ensure a consistent approach. Information about interest payments should be provided in client care and terms of business literature.

Where interest will not be paid, there should be satisfactory evidence that this is justifiable and the affected client gives consent. A template agreement, and COFA sign-off, will support compliance.

14. Rule provision – Client accounting systems and controls

Rule 8.1 states that the firm (described as "you") must "keep and maintain accurate, contemporaneous, and chronological records" to support the protection of client money. These relate to client ledger records, a list of all balances, and the maintenance of a cash book showing a running total of all transactions through your client accounts.

Rule 8.2 contains the obligation to obtain regular statements (at least every five weeks) for all client and business accounts.

Rule 8.3 is the reconciliation duty; this relates to your client accounts and the duty is to reconcile the statement balance with the cash book balance and the client ledger total. The record must be signed by the COFA or a manager of the firm, and differences must be promptly investigated and resolved.

Rule 8.4 is the duty to keep readily accessible a central record of all bills or other written notifications of costs.

Risk management

Depending on the COFA's background, rule 8 is going to be the easiest or hardest part of the Rules, but regardless it is essential that the COFA is satisfied that the accounting records demonstrate the safety of client money.

These book-keeping requirements are described in brief terms and the SRA has provided supplemental guidance to support understanding.[3] This guidance should be heeded, and the COFA will want to be satisfied that they have the information readily available with which to address any regulatory questions. The firm's accountants may be able to provide support with any upskilling the COFA needs. Whilst the COFA may not necessarily complete the book-keeping tasks that are necessary, they will want to understand the books and be confident that they are an accurate representation of the firm's handling of client money.

Careful consideration should be given to the reconciliation sign-off procedure. This is not assigned exclusively to the COFA but it makes for best practice that the COFA (possessing the necessary skills) does this themselves and does not rely on the assurances of others.

Case study

In 2022, a solicitor was suspended for six months and ordered to pay costs of £15,000 after it was found that she had failed to implement proper accounting systems, maintain accurate records, submit accountants' reports to the SRA, or carry out reconciliations. She had also not reported breaches to the SRA. The SDT felt that the conduct caused harm to clients and members of the firm. As well as the suspension, conditions were added to the solicitor's practicing certificate prohibiting her from being a manager or owner of a law firm, or being in any management or compliance role, or from holding or receiving client money.

Suggestions for systems and controls to support effective governance

- Double-entry book-keeping and properly written up records to show dealings with all client money and any business money relating to a client matter.
- Dealings with client money recorded in at least the client cash book and the client ledger.
- Having ledger accounts that are correctly named.
- Separate contemporaneous and chronological records of inter-ledger transfers.
- Central record of all bills or written notification of costs.
- Lists of all general client accounts, separate designated accounts, client own accounts, joint accounts, any third party managed accounts, and the firm's business accounts.
- A reconciliation process and a system for sign-off by the COFA or a manager with appropriate knowledge of the SRA Accounts Rules.
- Consideration of safety measures to support the duty to safeguard client money.

15. Rule provision – Operation of joint accounts

Rule 9 applies regulatory duties to the holding of client money in a joint account. This is in fact limited to obtaining financial statements at least every five weeks and keeping a record of bills and other written notifications relating to the matter on which the firm is acting.

The joint account phrase is not defined but will be used in circumstances where an account may be operated by the firm with the client, or with another third party.

Risk management

The funds held in the account are client monies but the account itself is not a client account as defined elsewhere in the Rules.

All signatories will have access to these funds, and so there are risks attached to the account. You will be expected to manage and mitigate these risks.

Suggestions for systems and controls to support effective governance

Training should be given to staff to understand what a joint account is and the information that must be given to the accounts team when a joint account is being operated.

Arrangements should be made to ensure that statements are obtained.

16. Rule provision – Operation of a client's own account

Rule 10 covers the position where an individual in the firm, or the firm itself, operates a client's own account as a signatory. There are three duties that apply to this scenario – statements must be obtained at least every five weeks, there must be a reconciliation exercise at least every five weeks, and bills and notification of costs must be kept.

As with joint accounts in rule 9, there is no definition of "own account".

Risk management

This scenario is likely to arise if a manager or employee is acting as a deputy or attorney and has access to the client's own bank account. It is essential in these cases that the manager or employee does nothing to compromise trust and confidence in the profession, or act dishonestly or without integrity. The limited duties in rule 10 are designed to manage such risks.

The SRA has acknowledged that it might be difficult to meet the requirements to obtain bank statements and undertake reconciliations. In these circumstances, guidance has been issued that you will not be regarded in breach of the SRA Accounts Rules if you take reasonable steps to record and satisfy yourself that the client's money is not at risk and to record the position.

You would be expected to keep a central register of the client's own accounts that you operate, maintain a separate record of the transactions carried out by you, and maintain the record of bills etc.

Suggestions for systems and controls to support effective governance

Training of staff to understand the compliance requirements that relate to the operation of a client's own account and the information that must be given to the accounts team when this type of account is being operated.

Arrangements to ensure that statements are obtained and reconciliations completed, or evidence to show why this is not possible.

17. Rule provision – Third party management accounts

Rule 11 provides – subject to conditions – an alternative way to hold client money that avoids the need to use a client account. The Rule allows you (i.e., the authorised law firm) to enter into arrangements with a client to use a third-party managed account (TPMA)[4] for client money purposes.

The conditions allow you to use the TPMA provided that you take reasonable steps to ensure before accepting instructions, that the client is informed of and understands the terms of the contractual arrangements relating to the use of the third party managed account, and in particular how any fees for use of the third party managed account will be paid and who will bear them; and the client's right to terminate the agreement and dispute payment requests made by you.

You must obtain regular statements from the TPMA provider and ensure that these are an accurate record of all transactions.

Risk management

This Rules provides the firm with a degree of flexibility in respect of how client money is held.

A TPMA can be used instead of, or as well as, a firm's client account.

The firm will still be responsible for ensuring adequate protection of the client and the client money in any situation where it is proposed that a TPMA is used. Therefore, whilst the use of a TPMA does enable the firm to disapply the Accounts rules, there is still a need to exert risk management to the alternative. The firm will need to undertake due diligence on the TPMA provider and justify use on the basis that this is in the individual client's best interests.

The due diligence exercise is necessary both before the TPMA is opened and during its use. The SRA requires "regular" statements are obtained. This is different language to the duties that apply in respect of client accounts and joint and own accounts. The COFA will want to ensure that this element of book-keeping is not forgotten with TPMAs and that regular monitoring is undertaken.

Suggestions for systems and controls to support effective governance

The firm's managers must make a decision about whether it is desirable to use a TPMA in all matters or for specific clients.

There should be a procedure and the production of evidence to show that the TPMA provider has been vetted. Template wording/documentation will ensure that clients are provided with appropriate information about the TPMA. Training of staff and appropriate supervisory oversight are also required.

18. Rule provision – Accountants' reports

Rule 12.1 states the duty to obtain an accountants' report if you (i.e., the authorised law firm) have:

- Held or received client money;
- Operated a joint account; and/or
- Operated a client account as a signatory;

during any accounting period.

The report must be obtained within six months of the end of the accounting period. The report must be filed with the SRA within six months of the end of the accounting period if it is qualified by the accountant. The requirement to obtain an accountants' report does not apply if you can show that:

- All client money that you hold during the accounting period is money received from the Legal Aid Agency; or
- in the accounting period, the statement or passbook balance of client money you have held or received does not exceed:
    - an average of £10,000; and
    - a maximum of £250,000,

  Or the equivalent in foreign currency.

Notwithstanding the carve-outs, the SRA also gives itself (at Rule 12.4) the right to require a firm to obtain or deliver an accountant's report in other circumstances (including the closure of the firm) if it is deemed necessary in the public interest.

There are two defined phrases to note:

"Accounting period" is defined in the SRA Glossary and means:

"The period for which your accounts are made up, and that:

a) Begins at the end of the previous accounting period; and

> b) *Comprises a period of 12 months unless you change the period for which your accounts are ordinarily made up or the accounting period covers your first report or a report after a break from practice in which case the accounting period may be for a period of less than 12 months or for more than 12 months, up to a maximum period of 18 months."*

"Statement or pass book" is defined in Rule 12.3 to mean the total balance of:

- All client accounts held or operated by you; and
- Any joint accounts and clients' own accounts operated by you.

Risk management

Unless the firm can rely on the exclusions arising because of the Legal Aid Agency carve-out, or because the amount of money held is below the financial thresholds, an accountants' report must be obtained. It must be retained by the firm unless it is qualified and must be filed instead with the SRA.

Suggestions for systems and controls to support effective governance

The COFA should consider the merits of developing a good working relationship with the reporting accountant.

19. Rule provision – Relationship with your accountant

Rules 12.5-12.9 deal with your relationship with your accountant, so that:

- The report must be prepared and signed by an accountant who is a member of a chartered accountancy body (i.e., the Institute of Chartered Accountants in England and Wales, the Institute of Chartered Accountants of Scotland, the Association of Chartered Certified Accountants, or the Institute of Chartered Accountants in Ireland) and who is, or works for, a registered auditor;
- The SRA is entitled to disqualify an accountant from preparing a report in certain circumstances; and
- You must provide the accountant with all information necessary.

There is a prescribed SRA form that must be completed by the accountant.

Risk management

The COFA will want to be in a position where they have access to the accountant and will want to be confident that the accountancy firm understands its duties in respect of the reporting obligations and the requirements in the SRA Accounts Rules. Guidance produced by the SRA ("Planning for and Completing and Accountant's Report"[5] and "Accountant's report and the exemption to obtain one")[6] will help both parties.

It will also be best practice to ensure that the accountant is appropriately qualified and regulated by a chartered accountancy body as defined in the Rules.

Suggestions for systems and controls to support effective governance

Again, establishing a good working relationship with the accountant will be helpful.

20. Rule provision – Storage and retention of records

Rule 13 states that all accounting records must be stored securely and retained for at least six years.

The definition of "accounting records" is comprehensive and means:

> *"All reconciliations, bank and building society statements (paper or electronic), original passbooks, signed letters of engagement with reporting accountants, the accountants' reports (whether qualified or not), any client's written instructions to hold client money other than in accordance with these rules, records and documents, including electronic records, relating to any third party managed accounts and any other records or documents necessary to show compliance with the SRA Accounts Rules."*

Risk management

The SRA is entitled to demand accounting records in order to fulfil its supervisory and enforcement work. Records may also be needed to deal with service standard complaints (and your relationship with the Office of Legal Complaints) and/or negligence matters.

The records must be kept securely; loss of data and/or accidental sharing of the data could be a breach of the duty of confidentiality owed to clients and former clients and also a data protection issue. Inappropriate disclosure of financial information might jeopardise duties relating to client money protection and also have financial stability and business viability repercussions.

Suggestions for systems and controls to support effective governance

Ensuring that this requirement is understood by colleagues who have data protection, archiving, and similar responsibilities would be prudent.

References

1 According to the SRA glossary, Financial benefit includes any commission, discount or rebate, but does not include your fees or interest earned on any client account.
2 www.sra.org.uk/solicitors/guidance/taking-money-for-your-firms-costs/
3 www.sra.org.uk/solicitors/guidance/accurate-client-accounting-records/
4 According to the SRA glossary, Third party managed account means an account held at a bank or building society in the name of a third party, which is an authorised payment institution or small payment institution that has chosen to implement safeguarding arrangement in accordance with the Payment Services Regulations (as each defined in the Payment Services Regulations 2017) regulated by the FCA, in which monies are owned beneficially by the third party, and which is operated upon terms agreed between the third party, you, and your client as an escrow payment service.
5 www.sra.org.uk/solicitors/guidance/planning-completing-accountants-report/
6 www.sra.org.uk/solicitors/guidance/accountant-report-exemption-obtain-one/

Chapter 6: Identifying, recording, and reporting non-compliance

In this chapter, we examine an important aspect of compliance officers' roles, namely the identification of breach events and what should happen in terms of next steps.

By way of a reminder, this responsibility is found in the SRA Code of Conduct for Firms.[1] Chapter 9 is exclusively addressed to compliance officers and describes the role holders' responsibilities as follows:

"*9.1 If you are a COLP you must take all reasonable steps to:*

a) Ensure compliance with the terms and conditions of your firm's authorisation;

b) Ensure compliance by your firm and its managers, employees or interest holders with the SRA's regulatory arrangements which apply to them;

c) Ensure that your firm's managers and interest holders and those they employ or contract with do not cause or substantially contribute to a breach of the SRA's regulatory arrangements;

d) Ensure that a prompt report is made to the SRA of any facts or matters that you reasonably believe are capable of amounting to a serious breach of the terms and conditions of your firm's authorisation, or the SRA's regulatory arrangements which apply to your firm, managers or employees;

e) Notwithstanding sub-paragraph (d), you ensure that the SRA is informed promptly of any facts or matters that you reasonably believe should be brought to its attention in order that it may investigate whether a serious breach of its regulatory arrangements has occurred or otherwise exercise its regulatory powers,

f) Save in relation to the matters which are the responsibility of the COFA as set out in paragraph 9.2 below.

"*9.2 If you are a COFA you must take all reasonable steps to:*

a) Ensure that your firm and its managers and employees comply with any obligations imposed upon them under the SRA Accounts Rules;

> b) *Ensure that a prompt report is made to the SRA of any facts or matters that you reasonably believe are capable of amounting to a serious breach of the SRA Accounts Rules which apply to them;*
> c) *Notwithstanding sub-paragraph (b), you ensure that the SRA is informed promptly of any facts or matters that you reasonably believe should be brought to its attention in order that it may investigate whether a serious breach of its regulatory arrangements has occurred or otherwise exercise its regulatory powers.*

One of the most difficult tasks is at 9.1 (d) and 9.2 (b) and is the requirement imposed on the COLP and the COFA to make the distinction between "serious" and other breaches. Serious breaches must be reported "promptly" to the SRA. Whilst the managers of the firm are jointly and severally responsible for compliance (chapter 8 of the Code for Firms), it is therefore clear that the SRA imposes the expectation that reporting, when necessary, will be undertaken by compliance officers.

Being made aware of what is happening in authorised law firms is crucial to the SRA's risk-based approach to regulation, which means that the SRA places great reliance on the honesty and openness of COLPs and COFAs. Any failings in this regard are likely to have serious repercussions for the managers and the firm, but in particular for the compliance officers. The SRA has a range of disciplinary powers that it can use against a role-holder who is found to have defaulted on these duties.

This requirement is a significant change from the position under the previous regulatory regime. For example, under the Solicitors' Code of Conduct 2007, there was an obligation on "you" as the regulated individual or firm to report "serious misconduct" by others. Serious misconduct was generally taken to mean dishonesty or other reprehensible behaviour. There was no obligation to self-report.

Although failure to make appropriate reports was a breach of this Code, there was little evidence that the SRA took action against individuals who failed to do so. Most reporting of serious misconduct was done on an anonymous basis and usually only where there were concerns that client money was at risk. The net result of the old reporting provisions was that firms generally escaped discovery and censure for non-compliance unless there was an SRA visit. It was usually a case of keeping heads down and fingers crossed if things did go wrong.

Since January 2013 (i.e., the "go live" date for the COLP and COFA regime), this position has changed and compliance officers will need to be able to:

- Identify non-compliance;
- Decide whether the non-compliance is serious; and
- Report all breaches which are serious to the SRA promptly.

There is no reference to collecting data about other breaches in this section of the Standards and Regulations. However, this should be done. Chapter 2 of the Code for Firms describes the compliance and business systems that must be present in all authorised law firms. This includes the duty at paragraph 2.2, which is addressed to the firm and states, "*You keep and maintain records to demonstrate compliance with your obligations under the SRA's regulatory arrangements*".

SRA Guidance[2] has a different emphasis and states:

> *"Your firm has an obligation to keep and maintain records to demonstrate compliance with its obligations (paragraph 2.2 of the Code of Conduct for Firms). We therefore expect compliance officers to keep a record of all breaches that occur. These records are a key tool for you in understanding the risks in your business. They should help you to identify where things have gone wrong and whether there are any systemic problems inherent to your firm's processes."*

Given the personal responsibilities and direct relationship that the SRA has with compliance officers, at the very least it should be seen as best practice to be involved in record-keeping and be happy with the way in which this is performed.

The SRA does not mandate how compliance will be achieved. However, although this duty appears to be expressed in a way that suggests that records are maintained to demonstrate success, it is perhaps easier and more usual to record breach events and by these be in a position to demonstrate compliance successes.

The SRA is entitled to ask for information about record-keeping at any time, and of course firms must complete and deliver an annual return to the SRA and provide requested data in this way.

It is important to remember that the COLP and COFA are not only considering breaches that arise in connection with the provision of legal services and client money, but also that there are more general reporting obligations. For example, we are told in chapter three (cooperation and accountability) of the Code for Firms that the SRA must be notified promptly about certain matters concerning the firm's viability, such as indicators of serious financial difficulties, certain insolvency events, if the firm intends to cease trading, and any changes to information registered with the SRA.

In addition, the SRA must be promptly informed of material changes to information previously provided about personnel (including changes relating to compliance officers) and if we become aware that any information previously provided needs correction.

In reality, this is going to be the responsibility of the COLP and COFA so it is essential that they have the resources and knowledge to ensure that they can perform this function.

How will compliance officers know what they need to know?

Compliance officers will need to have an up to date and accurate snapshot of the firm's compliance status at all times. This is necessary in order that they can fulfil their personal responsibilities.

Both the COLP and COFA will find obstacles in their way if they do not have management support for the openness that will be required or if they fail to develop an intelligence network that provides sources of information. This may require a "hearts and minds" exercise to convince everyone in the firm that they should not fear such openness and it will not result in a blame culture. The message should be that openness is an essential tool with which to support the firm's longevity through enabling a good relationship with the SRA and the ability to demonstrate compliance with the conditions of the firm's authorised status.

Openness will be made easier if the managers of the firm endorse such a regime through their own actions. Tone from the top sets the characteristics of the firm, and the SRA has increasingly adopted measures to show that compliance officers are to be regarded as one part of a larger corporate response to compliance. Chapter two of the SRA Code of Conduct for firms talks to the managers and, for example, sets the expectation that they will be instrumental in leading the response to the duty in paragraph 2.1 for "*effective governance structures, arrangements, systems, and controls*". It is likely that any managers who obstruct such developments will be censured by the SRA.

The SRA has further developed this thinking in 2022 with its publication of a research report[3] and its proposals for new rules which, if passed, will introduce explicit obligations in the SRA Standards and Regulations designed to ensure, amongst other things, that firms address wellbeing and unfair treatment at work. Watch this space!

For these reasons, compliance officers must ensure that they have senior management support for record-keeping and reporting. They must ensure that appropriate data is collected and analysed.

In all but the smallest of firms, or in situations where the COLP or COFA is not undertaking any other role such as that of a fee earner or other function, it will be a heavy burden to expect them to gather all information that is required by themselves. How will this work in a larger firm or a firm with branch offices?

It is necessary to have conversations and a plan to ensure information flows freely. Many firms respond with systems of delegation and deputisation as a means of building up an effective communications network and sharing the load, and fed through to them in a less personally burdensome way. In effect, this creates an intelligence network with the purpose of ensuring that compliance officers have a system whereby information is collected.

The table overleaf shows how such an intelligence network might work.

Record-keeping

The purpose of record-keeping is primarily to ensure that the firm is able to undertake various reporting duties as described in the SRA Code of Conduct for Firms. However, in addition to this, it is sensible to consider other benefits of record-keeping. For example, an ancillary purpose is to be able to have data to show that risks are being managed effectively. Do not forget the duty at paragraph 2.5 of the Code for Firms that, "*You identify, monitor and manage all material risks to your business*". The firm's systems and controls may include restrictions designed to ensure that individuals do not jeopardise the firm's authorisation by acting in situations that the firm has pre-determined are high-risk.

Here, an example would be a restriction in the firm's policies and procedures to restrict the use of information barriers to deal with the conflict of duties that arises in respect of confidentiality and disclosure obligations. Some of the most highly publicised court cases involving solicitor and law firm behaviours have been a consequence of clients' objections to the use of information barriers. Many firms decide to avoid the regulatory and reputational risks connected with the ill-advised use of such a device through absolute prohibitions or the need for consent of the COLP and with an adequate audit trail being created to evidence why the decision was made to use an information barrier.

Where a decision is taken to act contrary to such a policy, it is sensible to have some supporting records to show why the firm/COLP etc. took the decision to use the barrier. This helps if the decision is later challenged by the SRA, or even a third party such as the client or the Legal Ombudsman. Contemporaneous notes of decisions made are always worthwhile.

Table 4: An intelligence network.

Suggestions	Advantages	Disadvantages
Delegation of ownership of certain risk strands and the reporting function that accompanies the identification of regulatory breaches.	• The load can be split so that heads of departments and/or other senior members and/or supervisors can help monitor the effectiveness of systems and controls and keep their own records of compliance. • It is a clear indicator that responsibility for compliance is a firm-wide commitment. • Gives individuals within the firm the opportunity to develop compliance skills that not only benefit their own personal development but are a benefit to the firm by supporting the development of a one-voice compliance culture. • With the inclusion of HR and learning and development colleagues, this network provides compliance officers and managers with information to support continuous compliance improvements.	• Compliance officers will need to have confidence that delegation of this nature does not lead to inconsistencies.
The COLP and COFA attend departmental meetings and have regular communications with key individuals within the firm.	• Effective compliance is supported by effective communication, and attendance at such meetings enables compliance officers to develop skills needed. • Best practice information can be shared and discussed.	• Time consuming.
Creation of network of compliance champions within the business, delivering the compliance officers' messages and feeding back to them.	• Delegation so that work colleagues have easier access to compliance specialists. • Less formality will encourage more openness. • Development of a group of colleagues with regulatory knowledge and compliance skills will support the correct culture.	• Might lead to inconsistencies, and this structure will need to be overseen effectively.

As with the majority of regulatory requirements, there is not a right, wrong, or prescribed way of maintaining records. Instead, it is simply a requirement that records must be kept, that these must be made available to the SRA, and should place compliance officers in a position where they are indeed confident that, at any point in time, they have a snapshot of their firm's regulatory health and that they can comply with their reporting duties.

This lack of prescription enables the COLP and COFA, and the managers of the firm, to develop a system that suits their particular needs because it works for them. Issues to consider when planning to succeed with record-keeping requirements include the following decisions.

File-based or central records?

File-based records will obviously not capture all types of breaches or reportable matters, but can be used for breaches connected with services provided to clients or that otherwise arise in connection with the provision of legal services. Whether this is suitable system of record-keeping will largely depend on the size of the firm but it is probably going to be more onerous to have a system that is based on file-located information in anything but the smallest of firms. Use of electronic methods for the collection and centralisation of all records would be advantageous in that this should mean that information can be retrieved quickly.

Centralised or decentralised record-keeping?

The decision is whether all records should be maintained and held by compliance officers or should there be record-keeping by designated members of the firm. Again, this may well be decided by the size of the firm and, in many firms, the responsibility should be shared with other members of staff to avoid the COLP and COFA being overwhelmed.

The use of an intelligence network and delegation has already been discussed and this might be a way to decentralise the procedure provided, of course, that the compliance officers are satisfied that there is common understanding of what these delegated responsibilities look like. Decentralisation of this nature will only succeed, and ensure that the compliance officers have access to appropriate information, if there are effectively communicated instructions about arrangements.

Self-reporting by staff or file reviews and supervisory oversight?

If the compliance culture within the firm is one where there is no fear of openness and transparency, where there is adequate supervision and support, then self-reporting will be a way of life. This is essential if the firm is to understand all reportable matters (such as those relating to individuals in respect of out-of-office behaviours as well as matters triggered by unacceptable behaviours in the workplace).

Perhaps a good whistleblowing policy, or other notification procedure, which explains the reasons to why self-reporting is necessary (together with the importance of raising concerns about others) will support the need to win over hearts and minds and avoid any negative blame culture mentality.

File reviews, and effective and mentoring supervisory oversight, will support the reporting response more generally. These are good management tools and reviewers and supervisors should be made aware of what information can be usefully shared with the compliance function.

In other words, a combination of self-reporting plus sharing of compliance concerns gleaned through other exercises should be in operation.

Just STaRs breaches or all complaints data?

Keeping records of breaches of the SRA Standards and Regulations is a non-negotiable starting-point but should not be all that is recorded. Complaints data provides invaluable information about service standard failings and may also be indicative of misunderstandings concerning regulatory and professional duties as well.

Records of decisions to deviate from the firm's systems and controls

There is no doubt that it is sensible to keep these types of records. Bearing in mind that systems and controls are designed to minimise risk, it is nevertheless important that they contain procedures designed to allow for discussion of an override of the expected response should circumstances justify this. Such records will be useful evidence should the SRA or a third party ask for justification for a particular decision and they are also an indicator of effective governance in practice.

What information should be included in the record?

Nothing is prescribed. However, taking into account that the purpose is not only to be able to evaluate the success of the firm's compliance infrastructure, but also to distinguish serious and promptly reportable breaches from non-serious breaches, and to have audit evidence, the following suggestions should be considered when deciding what needs to be included in reports:

- The date of the incident.
- The date of the matter being brought to the attention of the record-keeper – was the matter promptly reported so that the compliance officers have assurances about openness and transparency?
- Who is the reporter? Is it the person who has committed the breach event or someone else? If the latter, does this raise concerns about the former? Are they trying to conceal matters or are there training needs etc?
- Brief explanation of the incident.

- The date remedied.
- The COLP/COFA decision about seriousness, with contemporaneous notes about why they have taken a particular view concerning the degree of severity.
- Follow-up measures – details of SRA reports, notification of other parties (perhaps the client and/or the firm's insurers and/or the Information Commissioner's Office etc.), other corrective or remedial actions, training, system improvements.

Identifying serious breaches – where to start

We have seen that the SRA distinguishes between serious breaches and other breaches, with the COLP and COFA having personal responsibility to report the former to the regulator promptly. This task means that the compliance officers' ability to make judgement calls about seriousness is crucial to their relationship with the SRA.

This is certainly one of the harder aspects of the role, given that the SRA chooses neither to define its meaning of seriousness nor issue much guidance about what this is in practice.

The reference to serious breaches was introduced in 2019 with the launch of the SRA Standards and Regulations. Previously in the SRA Handbook, compliance officers were required to report "material" breaches straightaway. It may be helpful, therefore, to remember guidance from the Handbook on the question of materiality as there seems no reason why this cannot be applied to current decision-making on serious breaches.

We were advised in this guidance as follows:

> *"In considering whether a failure is 'material' and therefore reportable, the COLP or COFA, as appropriate, will need to take account of various factors, such as:*
>
> *a) The detriment, or risk of detriment, to clients;*
> *b) The extent of any risk of loss of confidence in the firm or in the profession of legal services;*
> *c) The scale of the issue; and*
> *d) The overall impact on the firm, its clients and third parties."*

The role of the management team in dealing with non-compliance issues

The main purpose of the COLP and COFA roles is to give focus to the firm's strategy for improving risk management and, thereby, enabling an effective relationship with the SRA. This means that the role-holders have to work in synergy with the managers and owners of their firm in order to achieve their goals.

In terms of what the compliance officers can contribute to this relationship, regular updates and briefings about compliance uptake within the firm will help managers make crucial decisions about such matters as risk governance, supervision, and training programmes. These reports are likely to include analysis of file review and supervisory findings, complaints, breaches, and other indicators of non-compliance. Such information is essential if managers are going to ensure continuous improvements are occurring.

The management team is unlikely to become involved in dealing with specific cases of non-compliance that are minor or technical in nature. At this level, putting things right and dealing with individual responsibility will undoubtedly be a job for the compliance officers, with or without their risk and compliance team and other compliance champions such as team leaders and supervisors. Where the management team may want to be involved is in assessing more extreme matters that do, or might, fall into the category of serious non-compliance and also in new regulatory developments (such as, in 2022, advances in the SRA's interest in a firm's wellbeing culture).[4]

This is because these are matters that require immediate attention, and the ability to interact quickly with the SRA. With serious breaches, for example, a report could affect the firm's risk rating with the regulator and trigger a more active supervisory relationship and even enforcement action. This is not to be unexpected, being a condition of authorisation and, for the SRA, one of its regulatory objectives when aligned with considerations of protecting the public interest.

Failure to report will have far worse consequences for the firm and its managers and owners. The SRA is likely to find this an aggravating response in respect of what happens next, and an indicator of a lack of openness and accountability. Comfort should be taken from the fact that the SRA has demonstrated that it takes a proportionate response to breaches and to help those firms that are prepared to cooperate to put things right.

Some managers and owners, such as non-solicitors unfamiliar with the particular regulatory regime, may feel uncomfortable in endorsing and supporting such openness. After all, this need to self-report is a relatively recent regulatory phenomenon. Some individuals may be inclined to play down any breach or to take the risk that the SRA will not find out. Judgements about seriousness of breach events may provoke disagreement and tension between compliance officers and managers. This attitude will not do. The SRA Code of Conduct for Firms places specific responsibilities on the COLP and COFA to make prompt reports of serious breaches, so it follows that it is their opinion that carries weight and must not be undermined.

A sensible approach to deal with potential discord may be to agree the decision-making process as soon as the COLP and COFA have been appointed. Options may include agreement that managers are advisers only or that, if part of the decision-making process, to agree that if a consensus cannot be reached, the COLP's or COFA's decision is final. The management team needs to be sensitive to the fact that the COLP and COFA are personally at risk of censure if the SRA disagrees with a decision about reporting duties.

Compliance officers and their senior colleagues must understand that the latter should not place obstacles to the former performing their duties in chapter nine of the SRA Code of Conduct for firms. This is spelt out in chapter two of the same Code, at paragraph 2.1 (d), which explains to this cohort that they must have effective governance structures and similar in place that ensure "*Your compliance officers are able to discharge their duties under paragraphs 9.1 and 9.2 below*". Obstructing the COLP and COFA could take many forms, including not providing them with all information they need to make appropriate decisions, and it would certainly include any attempt to prevent reporting of serious breaches.

Common breaches

We have seen that the SRA has highly specific instructions regarding the reporting of serious breaches. What about common, but less serious, breach events? It is essential that compliance officers, and indeed the firm's managers and owners, are aware of common areas where there may be the possibility of systemic failings.

Understanding weak spots, common misunderstandings, and frequently made mistakes will help with the planning of systems and controls. For example, we need to be concerned about issues such as how many emails are sent to an incorrect recipient or with the wrong attachments, or incorrectly calculated completion statements meaning that we are left with small, but nevertheless, incorrect residual balances. Where these may not be serious as a one-off occurrence, regularity might trigger the need to reflect on whether there is a system failure and how best this can be remedied. Minor mistakes that are repeated too often, or without any consideration about how to remedy a situation or misunderstanding, could well indicate to the SRA that systems and controls are ineffective.

This reinforces the need for accurate and up-to-date breach records, of all breaches, and this will be facilitated by all work undertaken to ensure the compliance culture encourages openness and accountability, the message that it is not a mistake that defines an individual but rather what that individual does next, that supervisory and other intelligence feeds into continuous monitoring and improvement initiatives, and so on.

References

1 www.sra.org.uk/solicitors/standards-regulations/code-conduct-firms/
2 www.sra.org.uk/solicitors/guidance/responsibilities-of-colps-and-cofas/
3 www.sra.org.uk/sra/research-publications/workplace-culture-thematic-review/
4 *Ibid.*

Chapter 7: Compliance officers and international issues

It is important that compliance officers understand and accommodate the totality of their domain for compliance purposes. Where they are employed in firms with an international perspective, described as "overseas" by the SRA, then risk management, understanding, and reporting must extend to all outposts. This chapter explains the regulatory considerations of such circumstances.

For the SRA's purposes, the description "overseas" applies to anywhere that is not practiced from an English or Welsh location (on the basis that the SRA is the approved regulator of solicitors of England and Wales). Compliance officers and the firm's managers and owners must consider the consequences of this starting point in a variety of situations as explained below.

Occasional or temporary practice outside England and Wales

Individual solicitors and all others employed in the law firm and who are involved in "fly in, fly out" lawyering assignments, or otherwise providing services overseas on a temporary basis, must continue to comply with the SRA's regulatory requirements as if they were providing services domestically. They must comply with the SRA Principles and the SRA Code of Conduct for Solicitors, RELs, and RFLs, and where relevant the SRA Code of Conduct for Firms.

The SRA will expect your employees to be ambassadors for the solicitor brand and the domestic legal profession, and it will expect there to be effective direction of this by the employing firm.

Firms with an "overseas practice"

Overseas practice is defined in the SRA Standards and Regulations Glossary to mean:

> *"a. A branch office of an authorised body;*
>
> *b. A subsidiary company of an authorised body;*

> c. *A subsidiary undertaking, within the meaning of section 1162 of the Companies Act 2006, of an authorised body;*
>
> d. *An entity whose business, management or ownership are otherwise in fact or law controlled by an authorised body;*
>
> e. *An individual acting as a representative (whether as an employee or agent) of an authorised body; or*
>
> f. *A sole principal whose business, management or ownership are otherwise in fact or law controlled by an authorised body;*
>
> *Established outside England and Wales and providing legal services."*

In this context, the SRA-authorised firm is what is meant by the reference to "responsible authorised body".

Where this applies, the COLP, COFA, and managers of the responsible authorised body must ensure there is evidence that there is compliance with a specific section of the SRA Standards and Regulations, known as the SRA Overseas and Cross-border Practice Rules,[1] as it applies to the overseas practice and also by any regulated individuals (i.e. any solicitor, registered European lawyer or manager, member or owner of the overseas practice) who are "practising overseas". This is another defined term meaning:

> *"The conduct of a practice:*
>
> a. *Of an overseas practice;*
>
> b. *Of a manager, member or owner of an overseas practice in that capacity;*
>
> c. *Of a solicitor established outside England and Wales for the purpose of providing legal services in an overseas jurisdiction; and*
>
> d. *Of an REL established in Scotland or Northern Ireland for the purpose of providing legal services in those jurisdictions."*

The SRA Overseas and Cross-border Practice Rules are a truncated replacement of the SRA Principles and other parts of the SRA Standards and Regulations designed to ensure that the SRA has a proportionate relationship with individuals and law firms.

By way of summary, Rule 2 is the Overseas Principles, and a modified version of the SRA Principles that apply domestically to solicitors of England and Wales and all employees of SRA-authorised firms. The Overseas Principles are a slight variation to ensure that basic ethical behaviours are displayed outside of England and Wales.

Rule 3 applies to dealings with client money (overseas), another phrase with a defined meaning:

> *"Means money held or received by your overseas practice:*
>
> *a. Relating to services delivered by your overseas practice to a client;*
>
> *b. On behalf of a third party in relation to services delivered by your overseas practice (such as money held as agent, stakeholder or held to the sender's order);*
>
> *c. As a trustee or as the holder of a specified office or appointment;*
>
> *d. In respect of fees and any unpaid disbursements if held or received prior to delivery of a bill for the same."*

Again, this means that the SRA Accounts Rules are modified in a way that is proportionate to overseas practice but still manages risks that may arise.

Rule 4 sets out the reporting and notification duties that apply to overseas practice:

- You must cooperate with the SRA and other regulators etc.
- You must monitor compliance with the Overseas Rules and report serious breaches promptly to the SRA.
- You must also make a prompt notification if anyone "for whom you are responsible" is convicted by any court of a criminal offence, or is subject to disciplinary action by another regulator, or you otherwise have ground to believe that the firm or anyone for whom you have responsibility is in serious financial difficulty.
- You must respond promptly to SRA enquiries etc.
- Upon request by the SRA, you obtain an accountant's report in respect of the overseas practice.

Bear in mind the significance of Rule 4.5 to the COLP and COFA. Whilst the Rules in general are addressed to the overseas practice and to regulated individuals, the entity and these individuals are given the comfort in Rule 4.5 of knowing that reporting and notification duties are satisfied if they provide information to compliance officers on the understanding that they will report.

How to respond to this section of the SRA Standards and Regulations

The SRA recognises that the detailed domestic regulatory requirements are neither appropriate nor necessary overseas, and in addition the Overseas Rules do address local requirements that may influence compliance practice. Nevertheless, there continues to be an expectation that serious breaches will be reported to the SRA and that SRA regulatory reach will be understood by all regulated individuals, by the overseas practice, and by individual managers, members, and owners involved in the management of the overseas practice.

The SRA's supervisory and enforcement position is shown in various quotations. Consider for example, the following statements:

> *"We recognise the need to act in a way that is proportionate to the regulatory risks arising from overseas practice. This is reflected in the flexibility within the Overseas Rules and Principles, which are focused on matters which present a serious risk to the public interest and, in particular, on public trust and confidence in regulated legal services in England and Wales."*
>
> *"The SRA will consider action against a firm (alone or in addition to action taken against an individual) where there is lack of responsibility for compliance being demonstrated."*

In terms of risk management expectations, it is important that the following statement is noted:

> *"We would not expect you routinely to monitor client work or matters, or for any breaches to reported to us unless they show:*
>
> - *Systemic issues amounting to a serious breach of the Principles or rules (for example a systemic failure to protect client money);*
> - *Are likely to impact on the character and suitability of any individual solicitors, or those managers, members or owners that are involved in the day-to-day or strategic management of your overseas practice, to be involved in the delivery of legal services; or*
> - *Otherwise risk undermining public trust and confidence in the solicitors' profession or in legal services provided by authorised persons in England and Wales (Overseas Principle 2)."*

This requires an appropriate but, of course, proportionate response from the authorised firm so that its compliance officers are assured that they will have the means to be open and cooperative in terms of this part of the business. The systems that are in place in respect of the English and Welsh-based practice can be modified (and reduced) but consider the merits of the following compliance solutions:

- Ensuring that the visibility of the firm's compliance officers and any compliance team is adequate – will visits be made by domestically-based personnel or will there be local compliance professionals employed?
- If the employment of local compliance professionals is deemed to be the solution, will these individuals have sufficient understanding of SRA regulatory requirements? Is tailored training needed?
- If local specialists are not needed, perhaps local compliance champions should be appointed who become the face, voice, and ears of the COLP and COFA.
- Induction training relevant to overseas practice so the relevance and importance of the SRA is understood.
- Adapted policies and procedures to ensure consistency of regulatory approach.
- Regular training and/or regulatory updates from the COLP and COFA.
- Systems to ensure that the local senior managers are effective ambassadors of the firm's authorised status.
- Effective risk management communications and supervisory oversight
- Procedures for the capture of risk management information.

Other international regulatory issues

It is important to understand the difference between overseas practice and a connected practice. This is significant in order to demonstrate compliance with paragraph 2.5 of the SRA Code of Conduct for Firms, which is addressed to the managers and owners of the SRA-authorised firm and states as follows:

> *"You identify, monitor and manage all material risks to your business, including those which may arise from your connected practices."*

The phrase "connected practice" is linked to a very long definition so that it means:

> *"A body providing legal services, established outside England and Wales which is not an overseas practice or an excluded body but is otherwise connected to an authorised body in England and Wales, by virtue of:*
>
> *a. Being a parent undertaking, within the meaning of section 1162 of the Companies Act 2006, of the authorised body;*
>
> *b. Being jointly managed or owned, or having a partner, member or owner in common, or controlled by or, with the authorised body;*
>
> *c. Participating in a joint enterprise or across its practice generally, sharing costs, revenue or profits related to the provision of legal services with the authorised body; or*
>
> *d. Common branding."*

And in this definition:

"1. *A "body" means a natural person or company, LLP or partnership or other body corporate or unincorporated association or business entity; and*

2. *An "excluded body" means a body which is part of:*
   - a. *A Verein or similar group structure involving more than one body providing legal services in respect of which the authorised body in England and Wales connected to it is not regarded as being the body which is the headquarters of that Verein or similar group structure or a significant part of it;*
   - b. *A joint practice, alliance or association or association with the authorised body in England and Wales connected to it which is controlled by a body providing legal services outside England and Wales; or*
   - c. *A group of affiliated bodies providing legal services which is not managed or controlled by an authorised body in England and Wales;*

3. *A "joint enterprise" means any contractual arrangements between two or more independent bodies which provide legal services, for profit and/or other defined purpose or goal which apply generally between them, not just agreed on a matter-by-matter basis;*

4. *"Common branding" means the use of a name, term, design, symbol, words or a combination of these that identifies two or more legal practices as distinct from other legal practices or an express statement that a legal practice is practising in association with one or more other named firms."*

This definition is likely to capture the circumstances of many of the largest global legal brands in which, by a variety of means, an SRA-authorised law firm is part of a global network. Whilst the SRA does not have a regulatory relationship or reach over other parts of the network (because they are not an overseas practice) the common branding – or any other circumstance – which feeds into the connected practice definition means that the SRA is concerned about the risks of the association. The risks are likely to be most troubling if a global event has an impact on the reputation of the SRA and/or on the solicitor profession in England and Wales.

This interest and concern means that the domestic management and compliance officers must ensure that their regulatory position is understood and not compromised. Ways in which to ensure that this happens might include:

- Ensuring that senior managers of the SRA-authorised firm have access to the senior managers of the global business;
- That any global general counsel are familiar with SRA requirements;
- Information about risk issues are shared globally; and
- Any cross-border client introductions accommodate SRA regulatory requirements etc.

References

1 www.sra.org.uk/solicitors/standards-regulations/overseas-cross-border-practice-rules/

Chapter 8: Behaviours outside of practice

A challenge that ought not to be ignored by either the managers or owners of an SRA-authorised law firm, or the compliance officers, is the need to ensure every colleague understands the extent of the SRA's interest in behaviour outside practice. By this we mean both in our private lives and also in respect of personal relationships that may have an impact on their professionalism.

This is a proportionate interest, and one largely aligned with ethical attributes such as observing the rule of law, trust and confidence, honesty, integrity, and behaviours associated with equality, diversity, and inclusivity.

Some commentary from the SRA makes this point. The SRA says:

> *"We do not expect everyone to conform to a perfect ideal of behaviour outside of practice. The threshold for us taking action relating to conduct in personal relationships is high but may well be crossed by unlawful or abusive behaviour. For example, the exaggeration of personal attributes on a dating website is not a regulatory matter. But we will consider some conduct, for example using a false identity, as serious in this context as in any other."*

This may seem a strange example, but it makes a useful point. The SRA is likely to have concerns if behaviours outside of practice are more likely to bring embarrassment, or be otherwise damaging, to the solicitor brand. This interest extends beyond solicitors to everyone employed in SRA-authorised law firms. Damaging publicity, and enforcement work, can extend to interest in the law firm and what risk management systems and controls have been implemented to minimise the likelihood of such events crystallising. The legal press is littered with examples of disciplinary action that have been triggered by behaviour outside of the office or away from service provision issues.

Solicitors should understand this regulatory reach, and even be comfortable with this position, but perhaps we ought not be surprised if non-solicitor (particularly non-legally qualified) colleagues are unaware that what they do in their private lives could be of interest to the SRA and have consequences for their employment in the legal services industry. Educating colleagues should be considered a sensible use of compliance resources, and can be achieved through induction and regular update training, by cultivating an open and no-blame culture, by making it easy to discuss concerns and if necessary make reports, and to keep this topic in mind with the sharing of disciplinary decisions.

Equality issues outside of practice

If focus is needed, then consideration should be given to two particular risk hot spots – equality and issues relating to offensive use of social media, and equality issues and sexual and other forms of harassment.

The starting point is of course SRA Principle 6. Like the other six principles of ethical behaviour, it applies without interruption and demands that "*You act in a way that encourages equality, diversity and inclusion*".

In terms of social media misuse, guidance on this principle[1] makes the following point:

> "*You are responsible for upholding the reputation of the profession in your professional and personal life and for treating people fairly and with dignity and respect. You are responsible for making sure your personal views are not imposed on and do not have a negative impact on others. This includes expressing extreme personal, moral or political opinions on social media platforms.*"

The seriousness of this topic can be conveyed to colleagues in a number of ways:

- Induction training, which emphasises this principle and the crossover from professional behaviours into an individual's personal life;
- Managers being very clear about their expectations and acting in a way that encourages equality and diversity values;
- An equality and diversity policy that includes requirements relating to the self-reporting of social media issues; and
- A social media policy, which extends to commentary on the inappropriateness of offensive communications.

With harassment issues, there has been a worrying development that has seen cases of inappropriate behaviours between work colleagues. Senior managers are regarded by the SRA as instrumental to ensuring that equality and diversity values are embedded in the workplace and there are very clear statements made about behaviours that must be demonstrated.

The ways in which this topic can be discussed with colleagues include:

- Training of senior managers in legislation relating to sexual harassment;
- Ensuring HR colleagues are aware that these issues have both legal and regulatory consequences;
- Strict control of the use of non-disclosure agreements as a means to solve harassment complaints;
- Ensuring all staff are aware of behaviours that will not be tolerated;
- Reporting and notification process and a complaints handling procedure; and
- Sharing of SRA/SDT decisions to ensure that colleagues are fully aware of the extent of regulatory interest.

References

1 www.sra.org.uk/solicitors/guidance/sra-approach-equality-diversity-inclusion/

Chapter 9:
Personal perspectives

This chapter looks at the COLP and COFA roles from a personal perspective and examines various practical issues that need careful consideration by those individuals who have agreed to take on these essential roles.

The relationship of the COLP and COFA with the management of the firm

To be able to undertake their responsibilities in the way the SRA intends, the COLP and the COFA must be sufficiently empowered and supported by the managers of the firm. We have seen in previous chapters that the SRA expects those at senior levels in the business to support and enable compliance officers to fulfil their personal duties. It is essential that the significance and value of the COLP and COFA roles to the success of the firm are not down-played and that role-holders are not obstructed. This means that the management must accept that these roles, and perhaps more accurately what the role-holders need to do, are not some form of necessary evil that others have to work against, but that they are pivotal in ensuring that the firm meets its very wide, often onerous, obligations in the SRA Standards and Regulations. The managers must be on side, both for the sake of the firm and also if their own individual relationship with the SRA is not to be jeopardised.

An individual accepting the COLP and COFA role will want to have answers to some fundamental questions, which are likely to include the following.

Is the role full-time or part-time?

It must be acknowledged that for the COLP and COFA to have an effective understanding of the firm's compliance position, and obtain the information necessary to ensure reporting requirements are met, it is time intensive in all but the smallest of practices. The larger the law firm, either in terms of staff numbers or numbers of offices, the more that the role will intensify. This realisation will trigger conversations about how much time should be allocated to the role and whether resources will be made available.

Aspects of the role can be delegated to different teams or individuals, such as a dedicated compliance team, conflicts analysts, client onboarders, supervisors, departmental heads, the human resources and learning and development team, and so on. Notwithstanding distribution of tasks, the COLP and COFA must not be token appointments and the role-holders must have the time to have a proper oversight over the firm's regulatory position and be able to commit to the development of an appropriate compliance response. They should also consider the good sense of having the time to be involved in the preparation of risk management reports for internal use.

The danger of splitting this role with another function or responsibility, particularly if that might be of a fee earning nature, is that inevitably demands and pressures from clients will tend to invade the time allocated to the COLP or COFA role. This is particularly likely with the COLP role as that must be filled by a lawyer.

With smaller firms, such as niche practices, it may be that the role is capable of being undertaken on a part-time basis because the areas of legal work will be more limited and staff numbers will be smaller.

Should the role be held for a fixed period?

This will be a decision made to suit each firm's circumstances and the circumstances of the individual COLP or COFA.

There are several advantages to a fixed term appointment:

- If there are any uncertainties about the suitability of the role-holder or desirability for the role, a short-term period might be useful.
- It enables others in the firm with an interest in compliance the chance to progress into these roles.
- It will enable the compliance culture of the firm to develop.

The duration of any fixed-term does require careful deliberation. If it is too short, the COLP or COFA would not have the opportunity to bring about any necessary changes for their firm and may leave a job half done for their successors. If too long, they may lose interest and become less effective.

Should there be a deputy or understudy?

The Authorisation of Firms Rules[1] require that each firm has a COLP and COFA in situ at all times and approved by the SRA for these purposes. There is no requirement or process to appoint, or obtain formal approval, for a deputy COLP or COFA.

This should not stop managers considering whether it might be sensible to have back-up for the role-holders and for them to appoint individuals who effectively act as deputies. In larger firms, or in firms where the role-holder is also fulfilling other functions, for example, it might be prudent to have someone as a deputy who would be able to step into the shoes of the COLP or COFA, on either a short-term or permanent basis.

This may also be considered an appropriate role for someone who is a fee earner, or junior manager, but wanting or needing to become more involved in compliance. Without full-blown responsibility for the role, they would be able to split their time and develop their compliance skills.

Bear in mind that a firm must always have a COLP and COFA. Where unforeseen events occur that mean that a compliance officer needs to be replaced at short notice, the existence of a deputy does mean that there is an individual already possessing some familiarity with the role.

Remuneration

This is an internal decision. The SRA would not seek to be involved in deliberations on whether the role-holder should be compensated for their additional responsibilities but it may be a topic for negotiation when considering whether to accept these responsibilities.

When and how often the compliance officer should report to the management team

Of course, it would be impossible for the COLP and COFA to fulfil their roles without having direct access to the management team. Given that both parties have compliance responsibilities, there is a need for a joined-up approach. One function that is implied rather than explicitly demanded by the SRA is that there should be the collection and analysis of compliance data. This not only ensures that compliance and business systems are in operation but may well prove to be useful information to share with both the SRA, if requested, and with professional indemnity insurers seeking evidence of the firm's risk management.

The type of information, how it should be reported, and how often reports are to be produced should be established by both parties. Nothing is prescribed, but the type of information that would be expected to be reported routinely will surely include the following:

- A review of progress against objectives;
- Reports on lessons learned from complaints or breaches;

- Reports on file reviews and what they reveal;
- Supervisory intelligence;
- Updates on training needs and training programmes;
- Non-compliance events that have been categorised by the COLP or COFA and therefore have been immediately reported; and
- Records of non-serious breaches.

Other information that may periodically be included in reports could include:

- The outcome of any review of the firm's compliance arrangements;
- New risk matters on the SRA's radar and the firm's response;
- Any proposals for major changes to the firm's compliance programme; and
- Contact with or from the SRA, especially if this is of a non-routine nature.

In relation to the Accounts Rules, reporting could additionally cover:

- Residual client account balances – any issues and how they are being handled;
- The results of the annual accountant's report; and
- High-risk issues – such as requests relating to banking services etc.

How will compliance officers work with the management team?

A good working relationship with the management team must be established.

From the perspective of the compliance officers, this may mean having to work hard to persuade the managers that, despite any preconceptions that these roles signify yet another regulatory burden, compliance can improve the standards of professionalism within the workplace for the ultimate benefit of the business and its clients. This can be demonstrated, for example, by analysing complaints data. which are always costly and time consuming to deal with but are usefully analysed to establish root causes and dealing with them.

From the perspective of the management team, this may include having to accept uncomfortable messages about the firm's compliance levels and general attitude to compliance. The management team must accept that they are at risk of being exposed as part of the problem unless they work in partnership with the compliance officers.

Where there are pockets of resistance within the firm, the management team could be particularly instrumental in ensuring that recalcitrant managers or employees are persuaded to comply with compliance systems and controls. The bottom line is that the firm's authorised status is only as safe as its weakest regulatory link, whomever that might be, and there must be awareness of who that might be and how this will be remedied.

Particular care needs to be taken by a COLP or COFA who is an employee and who does not sit on the management team or automatically have a right of access to all business information about the firm, especially with its financial information. Without sight of the correct information with which to do their jobs, there could be adverse consequences for both them and for the whole firm. For example, if information about the firm's financial situation is not known to the COFA, then they may be unaware that action needs to be taken to deal with regulatory issues such as poor cash flow resulting from failures by fee earners to bill promptly or take money on account of costs or disbursements. This lack of accessibility could also lead to the COFA failing to report serious matters to the SRA in terms of financial difficulties.

Insurance and indemnity

Should the COLP and COFA consider insurance or an indemnity from their firm or partners to cover and protect them against the possible financial consequences of their role? This will be a judgement call for the parties concerned.

In terms of an indemnity from the managers and owners of the business, there will be both pros and cons for all concerned. So far as the COLP and COFA are concerned, they will want to be clear about what they want the indemnity to cover and the extent to which it is likely to be enforceable. Firms, on the other hand, may see benefits in offering an indemnity as an inducement to an individual who might otherwise be reluctant to accept a role but will want to be careful about offering an open-ended indemnity.

Insurers also offer directors and liability style insurance, which covers the COLP and COFA against the financial consequences of getting judgements wrong. It can be bought as a bolt-on to the firm's compulsory indemnity insurance and this might be worth considering.

Sources of help

No compliance officer should feel that there is no support or resources to assist with the completion of their duties. Internally, the COLP and COFA ought to be able to rely on the experience of their managers and owners and other senior colleagues.

Included within this group, for example, much can be gleaned from the role of the money laundering reporting officer (MLRO). There are many parallels between this legally required role and the role of the compliance officers. For example, when this role was first introduced it had to be built into a firm's governance arrangements and the role-holder had to ensure colleagues understood its importance and to embrace new procedures. As with the COLP and COFA, personal liability does fall on the MLRO in terms of reporting duties, with the MLRO facing the threat of criminal sanctions if their judgement is faulty. The systems and records that the latter maintains, the training in order to ensure the support of all colleagues, and the constant need to keep up to date with internal and external developments are all skills that the MLRO have developed and their lessons learnt will be invaluable to compliance officers.

Externally, support and guidance is available from the following sources:

- Regulatory guidance from the SRA website (www.sra.org.uk).
- The SRA Ethics Guidance service.
- The Law Society's best practice materials from the Society website (www.lawsociety.org.uk).
- From the Office of Legal Complaints (www.legalombudsman.org.uk).
- From the Information Commissioner's Office (www.ico.org.uk).
- By reading the legal press for disciplinary decisions.
- From the firm's reporting accountant.
- From the firm's professional indemnity provider.
- From external compliance consultancy businesses.
- From external training providers.

References

1 www.sra.org.uk/solicitors/standards-regulations/authorisation-firms-rules/

About Globe Law and Business

Globe Law and Business was established in 2005. From the very beginning, we set out to create law books that are sufficiently high level to be of real use to the experienced professional, yet still accessible and easy to navigate. Most of our authors are drawn from Magic Circle and other top commercial firms, both in the United Kingdom and internationally.

Our titles are carefully produced, with the utmost attention paid to editorial, design and production processes. We hope this results in high-quality publications that are easy to read and a pleasure to own. Our titles are also available as ebooks, which are compatible with most desktop, laptop and tablet devices. In 2018 we expanded our portfolio to include journals and Special Reports, available both digitally and in hard copy format, and produced to the same high standards as our books.

In 2021, we were very pleased to announce the start of a new chapter for Globe Law and Business following the acquisition of law books under the imprint Ark Publishing. Our law firm management list is now significantly expanded with many well known and loved Ark Publishing titles.

We are also pleased to announce the launch of our online content platform, Globe Law Online. This allows for easy search and networked access across firms. Key collections include the Law Firm Management Collection, Private Client and Energy and the Energy Transition. Email me at sian@globelawandbusiness.com for further details or to arrange a free trial for you or your firm.

Sian O'Neill
Managing director
Globe Law and Business
www.globelawandbusiness.com

www.ingramcontent.com/pod-product-compliance
Ingram Content Group UK Ltd.
Pitfield, Milton Keynes, MK11 3LW, UK
UKHW020916170926
8657IPUK00015B/158

9 781787 429192